GETAWAY

by
F. J. Whiting

©2000 by Jean MacKenzie

Canadian Cataloguing in Publication Data

Whiting, F. J. (Francis James), 1892-1937.
  Getaway

ISBN 1-55212-427-4

1. Whiting, F. J. (Francis James), 1892-1937. 2. World War,
1914-1918--Personal
narratives, Canadian. 3. Soldiers--Canada--Biography. I. Title.
D640.W564 2000   940.4'8171 C00-910812-2

TRAFFORD

This book was published *on-demand* in cooperation with Trafford Publishing.
On-demand publishing is a unique process and service of making a book available for retail
sale to the public taking advantage of on-demand manufacturing and Internet marketing.
On-demand publishing includes promotions, retail sales, manufacturing, order fulfilment,
accounting and collecting royalties on behalf of the author.

Suite 6E, 2333 Government St., Victoria, B.C. V8T 4P4, CANADA
Phone   250-383-6864   Toll-free   1-888-232-4444 (Canada & US)
Fax   250-383-6804   E-mail   sales@trafford.com
Web site   www.trafford.com   TRAFFORD PUBLISHING IS A DIVISION OF TRAFFORD HOLDINGS LTD.
Trafford Catalogue #00-0092   www.trafford.com/robots/00-0092.html

10   9   8   7   6   5   4

This book is dedicated to Eddie Heath, Harry Beaumont, Corporal Walter Turner and to all the others of my comrades who died in the "Great War."

Introduction

In the spring of 1915, when the sinking of the
Lusitania screamed across the headlines, 20 year old
Frank Whiting dropped out of agricultural college.
He left his Saskatchewan farm to the care of his father and younger brother and went - very reluctantly
indeed - to the hell and horror of World War I. Serving with his university corps in the PPCLI, he survived the battles of Ypres, Sanctuary Wood, The
Somme, Vimy Ridge and Passchendaele. He changed
as the dreadful years dragged on from a green kid,
"innocent, trustful and believing everything my
elders told me. After three years of war I was no
longer innocent; I believed nothing except that God
had died or didn't care. My trustfulness and dependence had given place to a well-developed ability to
look after myself. I was an expert at dodging parades,
guards and fatigues when out on a so-called rest. In
the trenches I knew all there was to know about
making the poorest of dugouts comfortable; how to
rustle food and whiskey from officers and others who
I thought were getting more than their share of good

things. I could tell the instant a battery or a machine gun spoke whether to hurl myself prone or walk on indifferently. To me the war was something to be endured, and, if possible, survived. At 23 I was an old soldier in everything the term implied - and little of it was good."

When on August 27th, 1918 he was captured by the Germans, he needed all his courage and resourcefulness as he set himself the task of escaping the stench and starvation of the prison camp. His story is one of stubborn independence and flashing humour, of audacity, a strange sympathy for the enemy soldiers he encountered and of friends and comrades lost forever.

Frank Whiting married his English sweetheart and came home to his farm and a career as a freelance writer. He died suddenly of pneumonia in the winter of 1937. His story is preserved in this book and in his battered, stained and faded diaries - testaments to human courage and the incredible folly of war.

Chapter One

The fire in the grate flickers cheerily, and the silent house is filled with the cosy warmth that is born of well-being and security and peace. Peace . . .
Outside an icy wind sweeps down from the northern barrens across the whitened prairies, and snowflakes tap gently, gently, like the ghostly fingers of dead men against the frosted window panes. Tapping . . . As if to remind me . . . tapping. As if I could ever forget!
My little family has long since departed for the night, and I am left alone with memories freshly stirred by a pile of old letters and diaries. Old letters, written in an almost indecipherable hand on a dozen different kinds of paper. Old envelopes, grey or green or yellow with a red triangle in the corner and marked heavily in black: "Opened by Censor." Old diaries, the pages blurred and stained with water. And some stained with a darker fluid.
As gently I turn the brittle leaves, memories steal upon me . . . the bitter gnaw of shoulder straps on a long, forced march . . . the terrible choking thirst during an attack . . . the unforgettable odour of blood-soaked khaki in a pain-filled dugout . . . the stench

of a prison lager . . . those hunted nights in the swamp.

The entry in a diary under the date of May 23, 1915, reads, "Decided to enlist. Last night, Dad, Mother and I talked it over, and Dad said if I didn't go, he felt he should. Then, of course, there was nothing else for it. Young Walter will drive my outfit, and with Dad to keep an eye on my place, production will go on as well as if I were home. I regret now the money spent for my winters at the Agricultural College. It will have been such a waste if I don't come back."

I didn't want to go. It wasn't so much that I was afraid of what might happen to me - I just couldn't work up any hatred or dislike for the Germans. But it would have been unthinkable for a young man of twenty to stay at home while his fifty-year old father went off fighting.

I remember that beautiful prairie evening so well. The sun was setting beyond the hills in a long glory of reds and gold. Through the screened doorway came the incessant hum of mosquitoes. From the pasture rose a column of smoke around which the cattle huddled for relief from the tormenting insects. By the deep window recess in the sod wall my father stood looking out across the fields, a stern frown upon his face. I was glancing through the weekly newspaper from which my father had just been reading aloud the account of the torpedoing of the *Lusitania*. My mother, torn with rage at the Germans, was wiping the supper dishes.

"Oh, the brutes!" she sobbed. "The inhuman brutes, to sink a passenger vessel and drown all those dear innocent children." Then to me, "If you feel you ought to enlist, I shan't say one word against it. The brutes!" And she wiped her eyes with corner of her apron.

I said nothing but wondered dumbly if the crime of drowning women and children was much greater than slowly starving them to death, as we were trying to do.

The next day being Sunday, I wandered idly around bidding a silent farewell to the things and scenes common to life on the prairie. The young wheat on my homestead suddenly appeared beautiful as it swayed and undulated before the gentle breeze. As I stooped and let the delicate blades slide through my fingers, a surge of affection for my windswept acres thrilled me. Stones that my father and I had dug out and piled with such labour, were no longer ugly and harsh. They were beautiful too! Rainwashed, their glacier-smoothed outlines displayed a wealth of soft greys and browns. A house, I thought, built from these piles would look fine. The gophers squeaked and flirted their tails, teasing me to chase them down their holes. The big hawks hovered and swooped in their continual hunt for field mice. A large mother-duck with trailing wing and frantic cries tried to keep me from discovering that her nest of eggs was just hatching.

To my oxen in the pasture I carried a handful of salt and patted their lean muzzles with more affection than ever before. For a long time I leaned over a rail watching the ridiculous antics of a litter of young pigs, while the old yellow cat, rubbing himself against my leg, seemed particularly appreciative of scratched ears. I noticed the weeds showing green on the earthen roof of the old sod house, and that the few hardy perennial flowers carefully tended by my mother, were already showing good growth.

My home! The home that my parents and I had built with our hands from the bare prairie. Suddenly I loved it all very passionately. Here were safety, love, peace. My room beneath the low roof that leaked streams at every shower, was comfort. My mother's armchair beside the iron cook-stove was the centre of my universe, and because I loved my home so well, I must leave it and fight for it far across the sea.

The war-madness of Europe had spread like a plague until it raged insanely through our sparse prairie settlements. The newspapers told of fiendish atrocities committed by the invading Germans upon the helpless French and Belgian civilians. Children had been seen with their hands cut off. Prisoners had been crucified. Boatloads of torpedoed fishermen were fired upon as they tried to escape from their sinking ships. If it ever occurred to anyone to audibly doubt the stories, he was immediately marked down as a pro-German - possibly a spy. "Liberty!" was the rallying cry. If the enemy won he would rule the earth. Certainly he would annex our country with her wheat fields, forests and mines; control our councils; make us salute the German flag and impose the Kaiser's portrait upon our coins and postage stamps. The idea hammered into our consciousness was that nothing German was good. They were vermin in human form, and any method that had for its object the extermination of Germans, whether man, woman or child, was meritorious.

Many of our close neighbours were Germans or of German descent. Honest, hard-working, friendly. Except for their strange names, they were just like us. We credited their virtues to the beneficent influence we had shed on them.

The next morning I left. Mother was very quiet during breakfast, but when Dad and I at last arose to put on our coats, she ran to her box of extra-special flowers in the window and made up a little nosegay of lilies of the valley and asparagus fern which she pinned to my lapel. I tried clumsily to stop her as it seemed a waste to pick them just for me. But she would keep on, while slow, heavy tears fell unheeded, as she carefully arranged the blooms.

When we drove away, rattling and bumping over the badger-holes, she watched us from the doorway as long as we were in sight.

On the platform, as the train drew in, Dad bade me goodbye and on a sudden impulse kissed me. He seemed all at once to realize that there was a chance that I might not come back, covered with medals and glory. I glanced about furtively, but we were quite alone. The touch of sentiment went unmarked by the neighbourhood.

In the train I unpinned Mother's flowers and folded them carefully in my diary . . . .

I am now in England. The sandy heights above the little sea-coast town swarm with troops. Hollow squares between walls of corrugated iron sheds echo and re-echo to words of command: Company will advance . . . Retire . . . ! Order Hip . . . ! On the left, fo-o-orm Platoon . . . ! For inspection, Po-ort Hip! (Hip being the smart soldier way in which "arms" are pronounced). Dust from countless lines of marching feet swirls and shimmers. Skin beneath coarse woollen underwear and puttees tingles maddeningly. Bugles far and bugles near blare calls unceasingly.

Odd hours, snatched from the grind, are spent in rambles over the countryside in an almost hopeless quest for a quiet beer parlour or eating house that has not already been spoiled by too many other soldiers. Hot crowded hours in a cinema watching Charlie Chaplin and Fatty Arbuckle perpetuate vulgarities. Peaceful strolls alone through an ancient churchyard, trying to gain from the mouldering stones a perspective on life. Trying, in this mad torrent of hate and blood lust to keep my feet on solid bottom.

The business of fanning the war flame is here much more intense than in Canada. The press screams with epithets hurled against the German. No term is too opprobrious - Huns, beasts, barbarians, liars, braggarts, murderers! I'm sick of hearing preachers call to Heaven for victory when reason tells me that German churchmen are doing the same thing. Obviously, God cannot oblige both sides. Who are we that we blandly assume our cause is so righteous that we only must call upon the Almighty to gain his support for our national aims? Who are these Germans to print on the belt-buckle of every common soldier, *Gott mit uns*? It is all very stupid.

The heat waves tremble and shimmer over the

Kentish hills. Up and down, forward and back march the columns of dusty khaki. Gnaw of shoulder straps, creak of new harness, stench of sweating humanity, echo of bugles.

Before a row of well-stuffed sacks hung from an overhead beam erected beside a newly-dug trench stands a drill sergeant. Red of face, mustache fiercely bristling, his breast adorned with the service ribbons of other wars, he addresses his squad of recruits.

"Nah, then pie attention!" (His accent is East London). "When Oi say 'Charge!' I want ter see every bloody cripple spring up orf the ground where 'e's lyin', race acrorss 'ere, plunge 'is baynit inter these sacks wot's 'angin' up, jerk it aht smartly and jump inter the trench be'ind. Them sacks wot's in the trench is supposed to be Germans too. Some of 'em's wounded, o'course, but any of 'em's likely ter stick a knife in yer guts if 'e gits a charnce so the safest wie is to baynit the bloomin' lot. Besides, if yer tikes any pris'ners yer'll 'ave ter share yer rations wiv 'em.

"Are yer ready? Git a good killin' look in yer eye! Nah then! CHARGE!"

Shades of Joshua and his murdering Israelites! This, mind you, in the year of grace 1915. And that fellow isn't an isolated specimen either. Some of them are even more blood-thirsty, telling us to avoid driving our blades through the ribs as they are easier to withdraw from the abdomen and that a good hard twist while the blade is still home will make a wound from which the victim will be less likely to recover. And this is only the prelude to war!

Our songs, literature and history have taught us that the words "chivalry" and "war" are synonymous. Is it because the Germans are such outrageously inhuman foes that we have forsaken our national standards? Or did we have any standards better than those of other countries?

Tonight I am thinking of the yearly fight on the prairie with cow-thistles and wild oats; of the crop of wild plums in the thicket by the river. I wonder if the flies are bad this season? And what are the prospects for duck hunting in the prairie sloughs?

Our first trip into the line was in a quiet sector by the side of the Somme River. A division of Saxons opposite. They had the reputation of being unaggressive and willing to let the war roll on as peacefully as possible.

Our officers promptly organized a number of raids which resulted only in an increase of sniping and shelling of our line by the enemy, a lengthy toll of casualties and a few pieces of coloured ribbon presented by the Corps Commander when we came out of the line.

On Christmas day we started to fraternize with the troops in the trenches opposite, but our officers stopped that, and when more Germans appeared in No-Man's-Land, shots were fired into the air to warn them away.

Our morale was low that winter. We had few guns and little ammunition. The Germans held most of the high ground from which they drained the water from their trenches into our shallow ditches. We were never set to digging good, deep, bomb-proof dugouts such as the Germans used from the beginning of the war. While off sentry-go in the trenches we crept under pieces of corrugated iron laid over a few sandbags, which meagre shelters were vulnerable to the smallest grenade or shell. Our press made fun of the pale-faced German prisoners as compared with the tanned, healthy complexions of our men. The reason was, of course, that they were kept down out of harm's way until needed, while we were continually exposed to the sun and wind - and the shells and bullets. Few of our trenches even had a *parados* or rear protection and in many places our support line was little more than a stroke on a map. In some places the front line had no other support than that afforded by a line of elevated earthworks easily seen and soon shelled to nothingness. These were called strong-points.

11

Dozens of murderous little raids which we launched in the dead of night with faces blackened and hands gripping trench knives were repaid next morning by a merciless sniping on our front line.

"Lead-swinging" or simulated sickness, was rife. As high as twenty-five percent of our rifle strength would report sick on the eve of a move into that deadly quagmire - the Ypres Salient. Desertions and self-inflicted wounds were fairly common. As a deterrent the long list of deserters who had been retaken and shot was read out to all troops on three separate occasions.

Spring of 1916. Deep within the leafy aisles of Sanctuary Wood beyond Ypres, a nightingale had his abode. Often on quiet nights I could hear his pure sweet notes echoing from Mount Sorrel. I'd whistle, trying to imitate his song, and frequently he'd answer. That was before the 2nd of June. I never heard him after. My company was in the front line that day, and about ten in the forenoon the Germans began a bombardment that for intensity was the worst of the war up to that time.

Two days later when the survivors of our battalion were relieved, we left behind us the flower of five reinforcing University Companies. Two-thirds of our rifle strength was either killed, wounded or taken prisoner.

They were Wurttenburgers who so thoroughly whipped us, and in my opinion a finer, cleaner lot of fighters never went into action. They treated our wounded far better than we were allowed to treat theirs - in some cases binding up our men and sending them over to us. Later, when they retired somewhat, they left two of our badly wounded in a shallow depression. A note pinned to one of them read: "We do not kill our wounded prisoners."

September and October of that year saw us in the "blood-bath of the Somme" as one writer has aptly described it. Here the whispered slogan "As few prisoners as possible" had the effect of a wholesale massacre of unarmed Germans.

Men who shot or bombed prisoners they were supposed to escort to the rear were never, to my knowledge, punished or even reprimanded. The prisoner-killer seemed to be regarded by the authorities as is an archbishop who drinks cocktails. Slightly reprehensible, perhaps, but nothing to make a fuss about.

The weary months dragged on. Trench duty, digging fatigues, drill, marches. We preferred the trenches if it were a quiet sector. But it was seldom quiet after we had been established for three or four days. Divisional medal-hunters would organize raids "To let old Fritz know who he's got for neighbours now."

At long intervals we received leave. Brief respites from the long expectation of death and the galling hideousness of war. Then back again. Drill, trenches and marching. High raftered billets, mud plastered. A wisp of lousy straw for bed. During one spell of fourteen months I removed my trousers to sleep only four times.

October, 1917 saw us in that ghastly welter of blood and mire before Passchendaele. My friend Beaumont who, despite my advice, enlisted and followed me, fell during the action. He often told me he was sure the war could not destroy him - that he would surely return. Yet he was killed. For three and a half years I was as certain of immediate death as if I had been a condemned criminal standing on a scaffold.

Spring, 1918, saw us with our backs to the wall and the wall crumbling. In early August of that year we bivouacked in the Bois du Boves, east of Amiens. While here we were told from Headquarters that the hospital boat *Llandovery Castle* had been torpedoed; that Red Cross nurses and wounded soldiers had been fired upon; that the battle impending would give us a chance to avenge that piece of German frightfulness. Throughout the army the word was passed - "As few prisoners as possible. Remember the *Llandovey Castle*! We don't want any prisoners."

Long afterwards I learned that the *Llandovey Castle* had been carrying war supplies and ammunition when she was sunk.

Such a kid I was when I enlisted - innocent, trustful and believing everything my elders told me. After three years of war I was no longer innocent; I believed nothing except that God had died or didn't care. My trustfulness and dependence had given place to a well-developed ability to look after myself. I was an expert at dodging parades, guards and fatigues when out on a so-called rest. In the trenches I knew all there was to know about making the poorest of dugouts comfortable; how to rustle food and whiskey from officers and others whom I thought were getting more than their share of good things. I could tell the instant a battery or machine-gun spoke whether to hurl myself prone or walk on indifferently. To me the war was something to be endured and, if possible, survived. At twenty-three I was an old soldier in everything the term implied - and little of it was good.

The war ground on - month after month - year after year. Trench turns, raids, spit-and-polish parades for visiting notables. Long, hard marches under packs weighing eighty pounds; feet throbbing with agony; shoulders a constant dull ache under the gnaw of the shoulder straps. Hour after hour! Dust and sweat and thirst in summer; rain and mud and cold in winter. Unabated discomfort. Total absence of privacy and the constant and most intimate association with men for whom ordinarily one shared no common interest.

During August of the last year the tempo of the war quickened. As fast as we came out of one battle we received new drafts and went into the line again. Casualties occurred so frequently that before one had learned the names of the new arrivals, they had vanished, and still newer ones had taken their place.

Early in the month three new men came into my section. I took up with them at once. They were a decent lot. The youngest - I forget his name - lasted a week. He was killed by a whizz-bang - an eighteen pounder of low trajectory. The eldest of the trio - he'd been a parson somewhere out on the prairies - hung on two days longer. Then he caught a bullet through the wrist. The other, Eddie Heath, and I palled along together.

Chapter Two

The entry in my diary for the date of August 25, 1918 reads, "Regiment lay in camp by roadside all day. Won 230 francs at Crown and Anchor. Heath and I volunteered for advance party going up into supports beyond Arras. Battle order."

We did not volunteer for the advance party because we were in a hurry to come to grips with the enemy. Not at all. An advance party being small may catch a ride on a lorry. Besides, there was always the chance of grabbing the best dugout and any abandoned stores or blankets that might be useful.

However, in this case, we were out of luck. The trench was barren of materials, and the only dugout was a deep, stinking hole with the entrance opening the wrong way - toward the front. It was bomb-proof though and of course we promptly settled in it. But with darkness came wind and rain, and when the company groped their way along the trench we were turned out by the officers who calmly appropriated our shelter for themselves. The rest of the night Ed and I huddled together beneath a rubber sheet on the fire-step.

Battle order!

As the "zero-hour" crawled nearer I distinctly noticed how free I was from dread or fear. Yet not ten days previously when wanted for an ordinary bombing party I could hardly stand from pure funk.

To the battle-wise old soldier a complete lack of nervousness before or during an attack is cause for alarm in itself. A seasoned hand, tense and highly strung, will ignore the thousand hissing, shrieking missiles bound elsewhere, but will fling himself headlong to the ground before the one destined to drop within killing distance can burst.

I tried to make myself nervous. I envisioned the enemy's curtain barrage coolly aiming at my body. I imagined the stink and taste of burnt explosives. I even pictured myself as badly hit in the bowels inching my way to the meagre shelter of a shell hole. The latter had always been my pet horror, but on this occasion I was utterly indifferent.

What if I did get badly hit? I had two bombs in my haversack. This would be my seventh big show, besides countless little trench affairs that didn't count. I felt the old law of averages was about due to catch up with me anyhow, and if so, what of it!

Thirty-six months of shell-dodging had taught me there was nothing in this charmed life myth. Sooner or later something had to happen. My number was up - I felt it in my bones, but strangely, I felt no dread.

The attack was ordered for 3 a.m. and fifteen minutes before that time the officers emerged from our dugout and gave each man a good stiff tot of rum. We then fixed bayonets and "stood to." Smoking or talking was forbidden, so we stood about in the bottom of the trench and watched the eastern horizon. The rain had passed over, and a few watery stars were visible. Just when dawn was paling the skyline our barrage opened like one vast battery.

As far as the eye could see on either flank the flickering yellow daggers stabbed the darkness. High overhead, close overhead, hissed and rushed and roared the shells. Faster and even faster they roared until the air above seemed full of flying metal and the earth in front a leaping, spurting volcano of flame and black earth. Then, as the enemy artillery joined in the appalling thunder, I felt my senses reel and grow dull under the merciless hammering of sound.

Presently the company officer, who had been standing with watch in hand, gave a signal, and we filed out of the trench. I noticed a change in the note of the bombardment. The barrage was creeping eastward. The attack was on!

Being in supports, we were moved up to the shelter of a low ridge just behind the battle line proper and after spreading out laterally in attack formation, one man every five yards, we were commanded to sit down and await further orders.

Heath and I crawled under the shelter of a piece of corrugated iron laid upon a few sand bags and a couple of boxes of hand grenades to have a bit of breakfast from our haversacks. Water was always scarce during an action, so we used it sparingly.

Heath was nervous. Every time a shell dropped near us, he'd shrink and cover his vitals with his arms. He seemed to have the jumps as badly as I had had during the last battle.

A serious sort was Heath - I believe he told me once that he had been a theological student - at any rate, I often saw him reading his Testament, and I must frequently have hurt him with some careless or cynical remark on religion; yet in spite of that he gave me his friendship. In age and appearance he was about the same as myself - twenty-three and a rusty blonde. A shell landed within a few yards, and we crouched flat while the pieces thudded against our sandbags, and clods of earth banged on the iron over our heads.

"Did you ever bayonet a man?" he suddenly asked when the noise had ceased.

"No," I told him.

"I never did, either, and I hope I never have to. If we get into any hand-to-hand fighting, I'll shoot from the hip. I'd never sleep again if I drove one of those

19

horrible things into a man." He eyed our rifles topped with their naked blades and shuddered.

From beyond the ridge came the steady clatter of machine guns, the metal, high above us, whistling like a million wings, storm-driven.

He went on musingly, "They told us down at the base to kill any wounded Germans we came across in an attack, as they were apt to shoot us from behind. Did you ever hear anything of that?"

"Yes, they fed us the same kind of rotten bunk, too, but I never heard of any wounded German shooting at our fellows after they had gone by. Moreover, I never saw any of our men bayoneting wounded prisoners, though on occasion we have shot them or put a bomb under their heads when they were dying in agony, but that was simple kindness and what anyone would do for a wounded horse or dog."

"You'd do the same for a friend, of course, wouldn't you?"

"Well, now, I don't know. For some reason we aren't so obliging with our own fatally wounded. I've often had to listen for hours to a man begging me to end his torture. Perhaps if I'd been alone with him I'd have helped him out, but usually there were a few of our fellows about, and the thought that some people might call it murder sort of sticks in one's mind. So, to avoid any argument and possibly to save my own precious neck, I let the poor wretch suffer."

We sat without speaking for a time while the earth beneath our bodies trembled incessantly from the bombardment.

"Look!" said Heath abruptly, "If I get badly hit today will you - help me out?"

I jumped as if stung. "Hell, man! Have a heart!"

"Promise me, please," he insisted.

"You've got nerves now but as soon as we start you'll be all right. I was as scared the other morning as you are now, and nothing happened to me."

"Never mind that, I want you to promise that you won't let me suffer needlessly if I get hit badly. Will you?"

"No. Certainly not!" I returned shortly.

"All right, then," trying a flank attack, "suppose you get a piece of shell through the guts, due to die some time within ten hours and no hope of losing consciousness until the last; all the water gone, stretchers all in use and we have to carry you out pick-a-back. What about that? Are you man enough to stick to it without squealing? Or are you game to shake on a little golden rule compact?"

Of course he had me, and I grinned sourly in surrender. We shook hands in silence.

"This, of course," I cannily observed, "only to hold good in the absence of a third party. I wouldn't want to let you in for a hanging, and you I'm sure, would be equally squeamish."

Just then came a whistle and a shouted order: "Prepare to advance!" As we scrambled out from our refuge, Heath turned and nodded his agreement to the condition.

Another whistle and a waved signal from an officer, and we arose from our places and walked steadily towards the crest of the rise. On the ridge, as we appeared, the enemy gun-fire redoubled, its range shortening as we advanced.

I glanced right and left and as far as I could see, our men were continuing in fair order. Occasionally one would stumble and fall and fail to get up again. My accustomed nervousness had not returned, and I walked along as if invulnerable.

We came shortly to the farthest line of advance made by the first attacking wave and we continued on into the German territory towards the village of Pelves some three or four miles to the eastward. As fast as we advanced, the Germans either ran on ahead of us or stopped and surrendered.

After proceeding for half a mile farther than the advance made by the preceding wave, the machine-gun fire intensified so that we could make headway only by short rushes between the bursts.

21

While Heath and I caught our breath in a shell-hole after one spurt forward, I peeped over and noticed that the advance appeared to have come to a halt. Seeing no reason for trying to do the whole thing we decided to stay where we were until the others caught up.

A machine-gun a couple of hundred yards ahead was sweeping our immediate area every few minutes. It was some little time before we spotted the place where it was located. Our shell-hole was too exposed to do any sniping with even a measure of security, so I wriggled back quite a distance and approached the quarry from a different direction.

My new position was farther away than before, but a low bank surmounted by tall grass gave me fair cover, and I managed to get away a few shots before being discovered. I rather doubt that I did them much damage as the distance was too great. Besides, my only target was an occasional glimpse of a grey shoulder or helmet.

Our spasmodic duel lasted an hour. Their fire either went overhead or, striking in front, sent the bullets ricocheting wickedly. Then my rifle jammed, and I crawled back for another.

As I was starting out again on my own little private war, the Company Officer came along and asked me where I was going. When I told him he said, "Don't bother with them any more. A couple of tanks are on their way and they will clear them out."

After getting back to Ed's shell-hole I lay with him awaiting further orders

Presently the tanks rolled into sight and at once opened fire from directly behind us. The shells from their light guns appeared to be zipping just above our heads as they clanked and heaved towards us.

We were hoping these tanks were going to do all our dirty work for us, but both of them stuck fast in the trench the Germans were occupying. The crews left their tanks and took that section of the trench and held it until we later connected with them.

About sundown we noticed the Germans massing on our left front, and as they started to advance towards us, a storm of fire swept across our line from the German covering batteries and riflemen on our right and left flanks.

The stuff was hissing overhead in sheets and I shouted to Ed, "I think we ought get back to the rest of the platoon and straighten out the line. We're too far ahead here."

Without pausing to debate the matter or to wait for a lull in the hail that snarled above us, he sprang to his feet and started running to the rear. Before he could get two yards a bullet smacked into the base of his neck, and he dropped.

Scrambling after him I grabbed him by the shoulders and dragged him to the nearest deep shell-hole where I could attend to him in comparative safety. The usual evening hate was now on in earnest, and the row was terrific. I remember hoping only that I could attend to my friend before they arrived.

Quickly cutting off his equipment and slitting carefully through the shoulder of his tunic, I exposed the wound. The bullet had entered the base of his neck on the left side and had come out at the point of the shoulder on the right.

It bled very little and after binding him up with our first field dressings I told him that he seemed to have a nice Blighty, and that it would not be long before it got dark enough to get him out and on his way to a hospital.

His pain seemed inconsiderable at first, and he complained only of a small ache in his shoulder. He commented on the fact that he had no feeling in his legs and a numbness was creeping slowly up towards his chest. He seemed filled with a frightened surprise that this thing should have happened to him, and to take his mind off the precariousness of our position I kept reminding him how good an English hospital would be.

"Ah," he said presently, "this is no Blighty wound!"

23

I was, by this time, pretty well convinced of the same thing. When my renewed efforts to rally his spirits failed, I asked him if he had any message to send to his wife, just in case . . .

"Yes," he answered, "but be quick!"

Upon the back of an old YMCA envelope I scribbled hastily at his dictation a few lines of farewell to his wife and two little daughters, in which he said he was going home to his Heavenly Father, and that his prayer was that they would all meet again in a better world.

After his voice died away, I tried to read it aloud to him to be sure I had it right but, soft-hearted idiot that I was, I choked before I was half through and had to give it up.

Meanwhile, I was glad to notice the German attack had been stopped just before reaching us, but as the machine-gun barrage continued unabated, we stayed in that shell-hole until it was quite dark. Then, when the firing had died down, I went off, much against Ed's wish, to seek a stretcher for him. My search was unsuccessful, and finally, with the aid of one or two others, we carried him on a rubber sheet to a trench nearby where he would be safer. I found him a shallow dugout and laid him there, but he complained that he couldn't get his breath inside it, so I dragged him out again. He was sinking fast now. The pain increased and he had much difficulty in breathing.

Presently he gasped out, "I'm dying, Frank - dying!"

I looked helplessly at him.

"The pain - is getting pretty bad." His agonized eyes held my own with a certain significant pleading . . .

Great God! I had forgotten our compact!

"You promised!"

Kill my friend even at his own request? Ah, no! A thousand times, no!

"It is dark - no one will ever know. Give me a bomb

24

- pull the pin - and go. I will release the lever - when I am ready." He whispered his plan.

No! No! Of course it would be murder . . . Yet he was my chum and I had promised . . . I would want him to do the same for me. He had been watching my face and doubtless reading thereon my craven scruples for presently he said gently: "No, old fellow - it wouldn't be right . . . We were fools. The pain - isn't so bad now." And he smiled as if to give me comfort. His words made me feel worse, if that were possible. We had made the compact; the need had arisen; he had asked me to play up and I had let him down.

While I was mentally lashing myself a field ambulance man came down the trench. Stooping over us he enquired if he could do anything. I asked for something to relieve Ed's pain. He gave us a morphine tablet that eased the pain for a time.

Heath was afraid that I would be called away on some duty and begged me, if at all possible, to stay with him until the end. I promised , and managed to get permission, although we had lost half our men and the trench was very short-handed.

I had to pillow his head and shoulders on my thighs as he couldn't bear to lie prone.

He kept saying: "Raise my shoulder a little - I can't breathe. Higher yet!"

The effect of the morphine tablet did not last long, and he began to get restless with the return of his agony. When the Red Cross came through once more, I begged another tablet from him, and as Ed swallowed it he groped for my hand.

"Good-bye, old chap - and may God keep - you safe!"

The stench of his blood-soaked khaki was strong in my nostrils as I gently pressed his clammy fingers, not trusting myself to speak.

He soon lay quiet and seemed to fall asleep, and while I knelt there, leaning against the side of the trench, for a time the star-shells and the rifle-fire faded, and I slept from utter weariness. When his weight on my cramping legs awakened me from my doze, I found that he was dead.

Chapter Three

Hardly had I risen to my feet when I was ordered on a ration and water-carrying fatigue. At Battalion Headquarters while we were loading up with supplies, an orderly came out of a dugout and, seeing our party, enquired if we were of No. 2 Company.

"What there is left of it." someone answered.

"Well, our old friend the Corps Commander has just sent a message through that should interest you guys."

"Spill the message and give your mind relief." growled the voice.

"He says to remember Stonewall Jackson's motto, "Press Forward!" A chorus of derisive hoots, curses and unquotable replies met the inspiring exhortation.

"Huh!" grunted the corporal in charge. "Let the pot-bellied old windbag come up here and show us how he means!"

Day was breaking when we got back to the front line. After getting assistance to lift Ed's body out of the trench I proceeded to bury him while I had the chance.

Dragging him to a shell-hole I scooped a shallow grave with my entrenching tool and hurriedly covered him there. At his head I drove a short stake and to this I tied an envelope with his name and regiment. Then I hung his steel helmet upon the stake to protect the envelope from the weather.

The morning strafe was well started by the time I finished my task, and as the Captain, our sole remaining officer, had told us to hunt good firing positions in case of an expected counter attack, I stayed in Ed's shell-hole, loath to leave him and convinced I could put up as good a defence there as down in the trench.

When I jumped back into the trench, the Padre was going through making arrangements to send out the wounded. I gave him Heath's papers with instructions about what to do with them in case I didn't get out to attend to them myself.

About ten o'clock, not being called for my duty, I took Ed's blood-stained sheet for a cover and curled up on the firestep where I snatched a couple of hours' sleep.

I was hungry when I awoke. I found a piece of candle with which, cut up and burned with a corner of sandbag, I heated myself a tin of tea and some bully-beef.

I wasted no energy mourning for Heath or feeling sorry for his family. Soldier-like, I accepted the fact that he was dead and carefully strove to avoid thinking of him or mentioning his name to anyone. My mind tried to heal its wound by ignoring the hurt. Whenever part of my intelligence wanted to grieve, another part - a ribald, jeering devil - would cackle: "Here today and gone tomorrow! His turn now, yours next. Hooray!"

A dry wash with a spoonful of water on my handkerchief rubbed briskly over my face and hands refreshed me considerably. After carefully wiping out my mess tin with a handful of grass I started down the trench to get the news. Every man I enquired for had either gone out wounded or had been killed. There was not a man left in the company, with the exception of the Captain, whose name I knew.

I came back then and tried to get a little more sleep, but the sun had gone, and it was too cold, so I lay and shivered.

About four in the afternoon the Colonel came down the trench enquiring for the Company Officer. I directed him and sat down to await developments. It was always a safe bet that when any officer of rank higher than that of major came down a front line trench looking for the C. O. he was not just making a friendly call.

It was not long before a non-com. appeared seeking Mills bombs. I asked what was up. He replied, "Raid at six."

We were to have been relieved that morning, but with a raid on our hands there was no telling when we would get out. We were short of ammunition and bombs. However, no one said anything. We all looked pretty glum.

Soon after, those of us who had been told off for this party were informed by the Captain that the trench we were to take was a continuance of the trench we then occupied. The German section overlooked ours, and we were suffering too many casualties from snipers. At six sharp our artillery was to open up on the enemy. Having gathered up all the bombs we could find, including those we salvaged from equipment abandoned by casualties, we then gathered at the block in the trench which separated us from the enemy section and waited for the artillery to open up the ball.

Six o'clock came and went, and no sudden roar of artillery. The only sound was the occasional thud of a sniper's bullet as it hit the parapet. Presently the colonel said, "I guess the order must have miscarried somehow. You fellows go ahead; you can do it all right."

I had my own ideas as to the wisdom of this, as the barrage might easily commence after we had started and before we had time to instruct the artillery. However, the officer in charge of the raid gave the order to advance and off we went, bombing our way up the trench.

When we started out I was about tenth in the line, but as the men in front expended their bombs, they, one by one, fell back until I was number two, number one being the bayonet man. I didn't know the whereabouts of the officer.

When we had advanced about three or four hundred yards without seeing more than one Fritz and he a stretcher-bearer who came towards us with his hands up, we topped the rise from which they had been doing the sniping. Those of us who were in front were proceeding through a deep section from which we could see nothing of what was going on up top, when suddenly from behind us someone yelled, "Run like hell, boys. They're coming back!"

At that moment I was busy pulling the string of a German "potato-masher" bomb - all of the Mills had been thrown - and paused long enough to throw it in the general direction of Germany. Number One squeezed past me and pounded on down the trench after the others who had disappeared. For a moment I had hesitated about running as I was not sure that it was an officer who had called out. However, I did not see any sense in trying to hold the trench alone so I tailed on after the rest as fast as I could go.

I passed the bodies of several of our fellows who had been hit as they ran over shallow places in the trench. Every time I went bounding over one of these spots I could hear the rifle and machine gun bullets playing steadily over it so that I was expecting to feel the tearing shock of a bullet plowing through me at any moment.

Our pursuers on top had a straight run, except for the shell-holes, while we had to follow the twists and turns of the trench so I knew we could not get very far before having to turn and fight. The trench was littered with abandoned equipment and German machine guns, and I could not help thinking as I ran that we should have been able to hold the trench, even though our own ammunition was exhausted.

I had nearly overtaken the others, just catching sight of them going around one corner as I came around the other when, topping another bad shallow place, I saw a line of charging Germans sweeping obliquely across our trench. The nearest was only five or six yards away, and as they ran they fired from the hip at those of our party who were still scrambling to get out of sight around the corner of the trench. The Germans cheered lustily as they raced down upon us. *"Raus! Raus!"* A hateful noise.

I yanked the string of my last bomb and flung it with all my strength at the nearest Fritz. As it struck him in the middle, he fired point blank at me and I turned and fell headlong into the trench. Before I could rise, they were on us, and it flashed across me that my number was up unless I lay doggo for a minute. The chap I had just tried to bomb would either shoot or bayonet me before I could get to my knees. I had no rifle or revolver, and my last bomb was gone. By lying still and feigning death, there was a chance that the fellow who had fired at me would think he had scored a hit, and the whole bunch might pass on. This I did, though I knew if any of them gave me a second glance they would see by my labouring chest as I struggled for breath that I was far from dead.

For the moment the ruse worked. The whole line jumped into the trench and as they ran on after our party, I heard the bomb I had thrown explode with a roar just beyond the parapet. As soon as the sound of their steps died out of my hearing, I came to life again, so to speak, and scrambled back over the shallow place and the parapet and began to work my way on my stomach through the shell-holes to a safer distance. My harness rattled as I wormed my way along, so I soon got rid of that. It was of no further use for a while anyway, as I intended to hide out in some hole until dark when I could go back and rejoin the company.

I had not snaked along very far when I heard the voices of the returning Germans. They sounded very jubilant at their victory, and I congratulated myself on having escaped from a bad mess so nicely. The sun was low in the sky and it would be only an hour or so until I could safely put more distance between us. But I rejoiced too soon.

Presently some of them climbed out of the trench to look for their casualties. I had not thought of this contingency and promptly shammed dead again, this time with better hope of success as I had now regained my wind.

I knew from long experience that the greatest danger to a captured enemy is during the split second while the capturer debates whether to kill or to give the poor beggar his life. Once safely past this instant of indecision, one's chance of being murdered in cold blood later is not so great. I had suffered a bit of a scratch on the forehead during the raid, and my face was smeared with blood, so when one of the Germans wandered in my direction, I closed my eyes and breathed very lightly indeed.

From the sound of his movements he soon spotted the "stiff" and came right over. He first investigated my haversack and then turned his attention to me.

By this time I realized I had made two mistakes: one in getting out of the trench on the side over which the Germans had advanced and the other in lying face upward. I may or may not have been pale with fright, but evidently there was something about my appearance that was unconvincing even to a cursory glance, and so it was that this chap started to investigate my "corpse." I did not know whether he would test me by sticking a bayonet through my ribs or what, so, to take his mind off any unpleasantness he might be planning, I flickered my eyelids, gave a groan and muttered, "*Wasser.*"

This was certainly a bright idea, and while he was trying to figure out what a man who spoke German was doing in an enemy uniform, I was slowly coming back to life and calmly ignoring what contributions he was making to the conversation in that language. When I had sufficiently regained my senses I opened my eyes, and when they met those of the big German who stood over me, I gave him one of my friendliest smiles and said "*Wasser*" again.

He smiled in return and answered apologetically, "*Nicht Wasser.*" Safe! I had won the trick. I smiled again, a real one this time.

After awhile, with the aid of my captor's strong arm, I managed to stagger to my feet, and he helped me back into the trench. To my surprise they all treated me well, perhaps because of my blood-stained face. That is to say, they did not go through my pockets for valuables or souvenirs, as many of our fellows would have done to a prisoner.

One of them fetched my haversack and was rather gingerly handling my emergency chocolate rations which I had carried for over three years. They were in a sealed tin, and I think he suspected a new kind of bomb. After solving that mystery and sharing my cigarettes with everyone within call, they returned to me what rations still remained in the haversack, also my fork and spoon. The latter utensil came in handy later on in more ways than my good-natured captors intended.

Then a sergeant beckoned me to follow him and he climbed out of the trench and started to escort me overland to the rear. Behind a small knoll we came upon a party of machine-gunners. The officer commanding them asked me in excellent English how many men we had holding that trench. I replied truthfully that I did not know.

"Oh, come!" he said sharply, "the war is finished for you now. You may as well tell us what we want to know."

I shook my head."I'm sorry, sir," I answered, "but I really do not know and if I did, I would not tell."

I hoped I looked as brave as I sounded while I told

him this for I fully expected to see him draw his revolver and shoot me there and then. But he only smiled and waved us on. We had proceeded a few yards when our belated barrage opened with a roar and crashed down all about us. We raced along in spurts, plunging into shell-holes whenever the rising scream of an on-coming shell would give us its hair's-breadth instant of warning. Several British machine-guns joined the chorus and the sergeant dropped with a bullet through the knee.

"Come on!" I yelled, grabbing him by the shoulder. With the help of my arm he staggered up, and we ran a three-legged twenty yard dash to the nearest shell-hole. Into this we tumbled together, lying for a moment in the bottom while we regained our breath. Bullets whipped in sheets above our heads. Shells shrieked from the skies to explode in leaping tornadoes of flame. The spurting fountains of earth and flame and black smoke blotted the field and the horizon from sight.

While I hastily bound up his wound with his field dressing, vagrant memory seemed trying to force itself to my attention. As I fastened his split trouser leg around the bandage to help keep it clean, I suddenly recollected what the drill sergeant at the base had told us.

"If yer ever wounded whilst tikin' back a pris'ner, shoot 'im. It's the on'y sife wiy."

I grinned wryly to myself at the grisly joke of remembering a thing like that, the altered circumstances being as they were.

As we huddled together, I toyed with the thought of snatching his luger from its unbuttoned holster and making my escape in the gathering darkness.

"Yes, you dirty quitter," I told myself, "You do a thing like that and leave this chap where he mightn't be found for a week and you'd deserve a firing squad. Forget that he's German and remember only that he's wounded, and you're all right. Your duty is plain."

The machine-gun fire slackened off a bit after a

34

time although the shelling continued with undiminished vigour, and I shouted to the sergeant, "Beaucoup Kaput here. Let's partee toot sweet."

"*Ja*," agreed the sergeant, and I helped him up on to his good leg and out of the hole.

With only three legs between us it was marvellous the speed we made toward an abandoned trench we could discern a little distance ahead. Part of the way we almost ran, part of it he crawled, trailing his helpless leg, and the rest of the way I dragged him. Then, in the shelter of an old dug-out we waited out the storm.

He seemed a decent, gentlemanly sort and made no fuss over his wound, and when we had recovered somewhat from our hectic little trip overland we chatted away as friendly as could be, in a vile sort of bastard French, which both of us could understand.

Now, as I have already mentioned, I had won some two hundred francs in a Crown and Anchor game the day before we went into action, so that I was pretty well heeled for cash. This money I had been carrying in a lined money-belt around my waist. In my left-hand breast pocket, together with my pay-book, a few photographs and a letter or two was my diary of our operations for the past year. In my right-hand breast pocket was a small folding camera, a roll of undeveloped films from the Amiens scrap of the week before.

While the sergeant and I talked together in the darkness of the dug-out, I pondered what to do with all this desirable loot. Although I had escaped being searched and robbed so far, it was only to be expected that before long I would fall in with a bunch that would strip me clean of everything of value.

After some little thought I put all the money and my diary in one pouch, chattering the while to disguise the slight rattle of paper as I made the change. I then worked the money belt under my shirt and shifted it around until the pouch hung well down over my stomach. By doing so I figured that unless I was actually stripped I could pass any ordinary search where one's pockets were completely emptied and the usual patting and feeling down the body was done. I did not anticipate a search that would discover a hiding place so low down in the centre.

When the shelling had died down somewhat, we climbed from the dugout and started slowly off down the trench to find someone who would look after us. After turning me over to a captain, we shook hands, wished each other luck for the duration, and I saw him no more.

I shall always think well of that sergeant though perhaps I did more for him than he did for me. He did not rob me. And when he was wounded he did not, I believe, even think of shooting me to prevent my escaping as he might have done.

The captain who now took me over led me down into a deep dug-out where he evidently had his headquarters. He could speak fairly good English and at once tried for information as to our strength and the position of our guns. Being balked by my ignorance, which he took for stubbornness, he presently said, "You are from overseas?"

"Yes, sir."

"Why are you in this war? We haff no quarrel with you."

"We have no quarrel with Germany either," I came back, "but nearly all of us are of British ancestors and naturally feel drawn in to Britain's quarrels."

"Hm, and what do you think about the outcome of the war? You know, of course, that you are losing? You haff heard of our grand successes in Rumania and in Russia and in Italy?"

"Oh, yes," I conceded, "you certainly beat us there but . . ."- and here I thought a little bluff wouldn't do any harm - "we don't consider you will beat us on this front."

He laughed scornfully, and then asked: "Haff you a knife?"

"Yes, sir."

"Then give it to me." I handed it over.

"Haff you another?"

"Yes, sir." (It had been Ed's).

"Then give it to me also." I handed it over, too. Fine, big, steel-handled army knives they were, and I hated to part with them.

"Haff you any more knives?"

"No, sir."

"What haff you in that little bag you are holding?"

"My rations, sir."

"Let me see them."He untied the string of the little sack and peered inside. It contained a couple of slices of bread and some butter in a small tobacco tin. He thoroughly inspected this, retied the sack and handed it back.

I looked surprised to have anything returned, for he remarked cuttingly, "We do not steal from our prisoners."I flushed hotly, knowing well enough to what he referred. This ended the interview.

The next dugout looked like a brigade headquarters. Five or six keen looking fellows were lounging around. One of the officers was sitting at a table making notes from a small heap of papers which I immediately recognized as British soldiers' personal effects.

This man ordered me to hand over all my papers, personal letters, photographs, pay-book - everything with writing on it. When my pockets were empty, and they were convinced I was not concealing a diary or other documentary treasure, he questioned me as to our casualties during the raid. On this point, I knew no more than he, if as much, since he apparently had the papers of those who had been killed.

They appeared to debate what was to be done with me. As far as I could make out it was hardly worth while sending a man to the rear with only one prisoner. They had no safe place there and to move me at that time of night - it must have been around midnight by then and pitch dark - was risky. The escort might get lost and land back in the front line, or I

37

might give them the slip. Anyway, as they talked the matter over I began to feel nervous.

Presently, after one of them had blurted out something at which the others fell silent and looked at one another and at me, he arose and pointing dramatically, asked in a hard tone, "Do you know what your officers do with prisoners when it is not convenient to send them to the rear?"

An icy hand gripped my heart, and my knees suddenly felt weak as the memory of a few ugly, whispered stories flashed in my mind. To gain time to think of a line of conduct I looked at him calmly and answered after a little pause: "Pardon me, but I'm afraid I don't quite understand what you mean."

"You understand well enough," he snarled bitterly, "I will put it plainer. Is it not true that you shoot prisoners?"

It was all up. I could not think of a good answer or even a good lie so I nodded my head and probably looked as much ashamed as I felt. "Yes," I answered gloomily enough. "I understand that under certain circumstances German prisoners have been shot. Not that I have ever seen it done myself but I have heard of such cases."

Perhaps I could not have given a better answer in spite of the fact that I was in a horrible panic. To lie was ridiculous. They apparently had their sources of information and to whine or beg for mercy was, of course, unthinkable. Our country, represented by my own unworthy self, was at the bar of justice. We had evidently been tried and found guilty of conduct unbecoming to soldiers and gentlemen in our treatment of German prisoners.

I felt it was up to me, poor specimen that I was, to keep a tight hold on myself and if I had to die for our collective sins to do it like a man. So I said nothing more but looked on, outwardly calm, while a few more remarks passed between my judges.

At the end of the short discussion one pressed a buzzer and two men appeared at the doorway. I noticed with apprehension that both wore revolvers and at a word from the chap who had addressed me in English, they unbuttoned their holsters.

A few rapid instructions, a short order and my guards saluted, about faced and with me between them, climbed the stairs to the surface. Well, I thought, I guess this is the last time I'll have to climb out of one of these stinking holes anyway.

After leaving the dug-out my guards conducted me along a trench for some considerable distance - looking for a nice quiet place, I judged.

As we stumbled along through the darkness, I weighed the chances of escape. If I attacked my escort and was later recaptured, I knew what to expect without delay. At the same time I had no intention of being led off and shot like a sick sheep. They could only kill me once, but I would put off the moment as long as I possibly could.

They could not do the deed in the trench. I felt certain of that if only because of the trouble I'd be to hoist out and dispose of afterwards. If there was going to be any dirty work, they would take me out of the trench and over to some good deep shell-hole where they would not even have to bury me.

I decided that as soon as the lead man left the trench I would make my bid for freedom. Scrambling after him, I would throw a handful of dirt in the eyes of the one behind me, trip the other with a sudden tackle and dodge off taking a chance with the revolver bullets in the darkness.

The trench began to get shallow and at a low place beside a dugout entrance the German in front clambered up to the level. I gathered myself and grabbing a handful of clay crushed it fine while apparently fumbling for a foothold. Now! I swung back my arm to hurl the dirt when a man spoke from the dugout entrance. I checked myself and peered forward. He seemed to be on gas-guard and held a rifle in his hands.

Chapter Four

The rifle was bad. A man running in the dark from a revolver fired from his own level has a fair chance of escape, but to run from a man with a rifle who can sight above the sky-line - that is a different matter.
The three Germans jabbered together for several minutes, while I sought to readjust my plan. Before I could decide on anything, the man on top jumped back into the trench and with his companion returned the way we had come leaving me with the gas-sentry, who motioned me down into the dugout.
The stairs were crowded with soldiery sitting or sprawling upon the steps all trying to get a little sleep. One of them turned a flashlight on me, as I carefully picked my way down to the bottom. Here I waited for a little time, the chill in my heart slowly receding as I came to the conclusion that the proposed execution had in some way fizzled out.
After a moment the German on the bottom step struck a match and squeezing over motioned me to a seat beside him. An orderly in the captain's dugout who had taken my knives had slipped me a couple of cigars, and these I now brought out, and my companion and I proceeded to smoke them. They were very good, being quite mild. After the smoke,

the Fritz gave me a handful of little white biscuits. They were sweeter than our army biscuits but not so nourishing.

We sat there the rest of the night. Sometimes I would doze with my head on his shoulder, and again he would drop off with his head on me, but our seats were very hard and uncomfortable, and for the most part we just sat.

About dawn everyone was called to the surface. Our barrage was on, and another attack was either under way or expected. My "bed-fellow" on the stairs bade me goodbye and remarked something to the effect that it was better to be a prisoner than to be killed in the trenches. I thought of my narrow squeak the previous night and grinned in agreement. I felt I could now afford to grin. If there was going to be any execution, I was sure it would not have been put off until now.

A mounted escort armed with a lance led me several miles to the rear leaving me at a French chateau which appeared to be an artillery corps headquarters.

I was held here for several hours. One of the cooks gave me a good meal of some rich soup and sour brown bread. The bread seemed to be the regular army issue, but I could not down it. Later, though, I came to think that same sour bread had a more delicious flavour than the finest cake or pastry I had ever tasted. Several of the men gave me cigars, and one directed me to a comfortable place under a tree where I could rest.

A considerable number of officers were quartered here. None of these, however, so much as glanced in my direction. Nearly all wore long field-grey overcoats of beautiful material over well-pressed long trousers. Their shoes were of excellent quality and very stylish. Those who did not wear smart caps sported handsome black helmets ornamented with gilt spikes and eagles.

To each other they practised admirable courtliness.

When greeting a new-comer to a group all would jerk to attention, click their heels, salute and bow stiffly from the hips. Not a deep bow but a quick bend forward. A gracious, lordly crew.

About four in the afternoon another Uhlan took me in charge, and on we went again. This man was an out-and-out Socialist, and our ideas on the war - why it was allowed to begin and the probable final outcome agreed pretty well on the whole. He thought neither side would ultimately win, but that all would mutually drop the struggle through exhaustion. I disagreed with him on that point, as it seemed to me the professional flag-wavers of both sides would insist on a decision of sorts that would at least appear as a victory.

The roads and towns teemed with the field-grey legions. Every estaminet and shop was crowded with soldiery. Nearly every house bore a notice in German telling the number of men that could be billeted there. Hardly a wall which did not bear large sign-boards indicating the direction to dressing stations, motor parks, farriers, supply dumps and a thousand other such places. The few small signs in French seemed swamped.

And westward swung the long columns of infantry as they trudged up the line. Like our fellows they appeared none too cheerful at the prospect, though there was a little singing as they marched along. One song which seemed very popular had a trick of suddenly breaking off and the men would march silently — One — Two — Three — Four — singing again for a little only to break off suddenly again. I never did learn what it was about.

Now and again a voice would call from the passing files, "Hi, Tommee, long way Tipperary, vot?" At this sally his companions never failed to chuckle appreciatively, while I grinned in reply. They seemed to relish keenly the thought that we had found it a long way.

The civilians were very much in awe and fear of

all who wore the German uniform. Those who spoke to me or offered me food kept glancing timidly at my escort as if expecting a sudden blow or at least a very loud bellow.

One of the first characteristics of the German soldier was the habit of bellowing at the slightest provocation. The officers roared at the NCOs; the non-coms bellowed at the men, and the whole army united in roaring and bellowing at the civilians. It occurred to me that there was something about the German language that seemed to lend itself to invective. A bawling out in *Deutsch* sounds infinitely more devastating than in other languages.

If a military policeman saw a civilian giving me bread or speaking to me he would rush up and cuff the civvy - either male or female, bluster at the escort, call down maledictions upon us from above and beneath the earth, cuff the civilian again and give the escort and me a hearty shove of dismissal. The MPs appeared to be as thoroughly detested on the German as they were on our side of the line.

About sundown we came to a mining town named Sin-le-Noble. Here my Uhlan paused to enquire his way of some of the townsfolk, who at once crowded around. While one or two answered his queries, the rest shot an eager volley of questions at me to learn how the war was really going.

The Germans had that day been moving back some of their long-range guns and were mounting them beneath the trees that bordered a neighbouring canal. The Germans denied that they were retiring even a little, but the French thought it a hopeful sign and were checking up their own observations with my recent firing-line knowledge.

They all crowded around, and the Uhlan had to get pretty snappy with them in order to keep command of the situation. They did so want to know when I thought the war would be over - fairly pleading with me to say "soon," which of course I did as a little renewed hope would do them no harm. Finally the Uhlan delivered me at a house where a number of NCO's were playing cards.

For an hour or more I was made to stand there while they finished their game, went into conference as to what should be done with me and sent for a guard to take me away.

In the meantime the woman of the house in which these Germans were billeted began to prepare supper. She took great interest in me and collected a large plate of special tidbits from her larder for my benefit. She had little enough for herself, but of what she had I was to get the best. Placing the food on a small shelf nearby she motioned me to help myself, but those at the table interposed with surly growls and refused to let me eat it.

While she had been bustling about, several other women came in one by one and pretended to help around the kitchen though they spent most of their time carrying on a whispered conversation with me. One of them, a fine looking girl of about twenty, watched me steadily, although she stood quietly in the background saying but little to anyone.

"Couches-ici ce soir?" asked one of the older women of me - an impish, little dark thing.

"Peut-être," I told her. I didn't care where I slept so long as it was soon.

Then with a wicked giggle, "Avec Mademoiselle là, ah oui, très bon?" She nodded her head toward the girl I had previously noticed, who laughed a little and made a face at my questioner.

This was coming it a bit blunt for a modest violet like myself; still, when in Rome . . .

"You had better ask the Boches," I chuckled.

Not in the least backward she promptly did so, and they as promptly squashed her thoughtful suggestion for my comfort with a few well chosen, though roughly expressed remarks.

These unexpected moral scruples on the part of my chaperons put something of a damper on the party at our end of the room, and they fell silent then, each apparently pondering ways and means.

Before the problem had been solved my escort arrived, a disagreeable Teuton dressed up in a spiked helmet, equipment, side arms and a rifle. After he had been given instructions where to take me, he turned to the door nodding to me to follow. At that moment I felt a velvety arm encircle my neck from behind and a pair of soft, warm lips crushed themselves to mine. It was the girl.

At the time I would infinitely have preferred something to eat, but one eats lots of food during a lifetime and forgets most of it. On the other hand, a kiss like that . . .

About midnight we arrived at the little town of Lewarde where an officer took me in charge. In faultless English, embellished with a near-Oxford accent, he also enquired as to the approximate casualties during the previous two or three weeks' fighting, but this I did not know. He asked the number of machine-guns to each platoon. I did not even know that. In fact he asked questions for half an hour or more, and it was nothing less than amazing the amount I didn't know. Finally he laughed and turning around looked me full in the face for the first time.

"You'll do," he remarked; then on a sudden thought, "When did you eat last?"

"Not since noon," I told him hopefully.

My hope was hardly justified for he fetched me some of their sour brown bread. I made a noble attempt to eat it, and although he gave me some honey to spread on it, about two mouthfuls was all I could manage.

He then directed me into a small adjoining outhouse where I curled up on some shavings to get a little sleep at last. I had lost count of the days and nights that had passed since I had a proper sleep. I only knew that my eyes stung like fire, and my brain and body were numb with fatigue, but my luck was out. The shavings simply crawled with fleas!

All my life I have been noted as a dainty morsel

for fleas and such like beasts of prey, and when the skirmishers of the flea army sampled me and spread the glad tidings to the rest they all swarmed in and a right merry time they had. Scratching, writhing and groping, the rest of the night was barely endured.

Towards morning, three Imperials (English troops) were brought in, and until daylight we shared both the shavings and the fleas as good comrades should.

After a breakfast of a piece of black bread helped down with some warm, dark stuff that the guard called coffee, I enquired if we could get a wash. Obligingly the guard obtained permission to take us down the street a little way to a pump.

My socks had not been off my feet since before the battle and I was very foot-sore so I asked a French woman who was watching us if she could sell me a clean pair of socks. For answer she ran in and fetched a pair of black ones but would not take a sou in payment. Another woman brought us a bowl and another soap and towels and told us to keep them. Quite a little group gathered around, and all seemed to want to do something for us.

Then the guard took us back to the shavings and the fleas among which we passed the time until noon, when our guard brought us each a large tinful of good, rich stew. The best, in fact, I was to get until I again visited the Intelligence Bureau.

The portion of the house occupied by Madame and her daughter opened at the rear into a tiny walled-in court yard. The door of the guard-room or prisoner's coop also opened into the yard, and we had the run of this while under the eye of the sentry. The sentries were changed every couple of hours, and like most human beings, some were easy-going and some were not. The easy-going ones would allow Madame to talk to me - so long as no officer was in sight or hearing - and from this poor woman I began to get some idea of what the war had meant to the "civiles" on the German side of the line.

She told me her husband and son had been called

47

to the colours early in August, 1914. How the German army had arrived a few days later and settled down upon all the land and upon every household like a huge iron hand. From that day she had heard no word of her men-folk. Nor had it been possible to get word to them telling how they were faring under the German occupation.

I was just giving her what comfort I could think of in the way of hopeful news, when the sentry ordered Madame into the house and me back to the coop. Well, I reflected, our women had it bad enough, but most of them, at any rate, could keep in touch with their men and certainly were not compelled to entertain a houseful of enemy soldiers for four years.

During the day other prisoners trickled in, and when we numbered about a dozen, they marched us all up to Douai where we lodged in an improvised prison which in happier days had been the local Bank of France. Two or three hundred newly-captured prisoners were held there continually. More arrived every few hours by day and night, and every two or three days drafts of a hundred or so were sent from this place to working camps of different sorts all over this part of France.

There were no fatigue parties or work of any sort to do in this camp, and by the judicious use of a couple of francs I bribed my way to an upstairs room containing only seven other occupants. Here, upon a vacant spring bed with mattress and a blanket, I held my headquarters for the three subsequent days, emerging only for roll-call and meals and sleeping a full eighteen hours a day.

While here a tall, dark German came through the building one day announcing that any of us who had French money should hand it over to him and he would get it exchanged. As my French money was not of much use to me now, I gave him all I had though I fully expected to get well rooked. However my suspicions were quite unjustified, as he presently reappeared and in exchange for my two hundred francs he returned me about a hundred and seventy marks which at that time was a fair enough exchange. He accounted for every sou in a very businesslike manner and did not charge me anything for the accommodation.

After about three days' sojourn at Douai, about a hundred of us were numbered off to move elsewhere as the bank was growing over-crowded. I happened to be in the number, and we were marched down to the station and loaded into third-class carriages. A couple of hours later we detrained at Vallenciennes and were marched north as far as Conde, an old walled town close to the border between France and Belgium.

It was quite dark when we arrived at our destination, and we had a deuce of a time finding our way about and getting settled for the night. The ground floor was all taken up with horse stalls. After an hour of groping around in the pitch dark, falling over legs, bumping into walls and nearly breaking my neck down some stairs I finally gave up trying to find a mattress or unoccupied blanket and curled up for the rest of the night on the stone floor. Nothing for a pillow, no overcoat or covering whatsoever. I thought it was surely a cruel war.

The following morning we were all paraded in two long lines and counted. No small chore that, as the cavalry barracks in which we were lodged now held between six and seven hundred men. Every few minutes a late comer or two would sneak in from behind and upset the formation. After horrible cursing on the part of the German sergeant in charge, he took himself off apparently more or less satisfied with the tally, and we were given breakfast, one-seventh of a loaf of bread to each man. There was a mess-tin half filled with what was called tea.

Someone later told me the tea was made from an infusion of beech leaves. Leaves of some sort they certainly were, but not tea leaves. No sugar nor milk, nor butter, nor jam nor anything else but a small piece of bread and this "tea." We were then dismissed, and I hied me forth to hunt a bed. I finally spotted one chap who was lying on two mattresses, and after a bit of an argument he came across and shared up. I was just starting out to find a blanket, when the interpreter came in and announced that all of us who arrived the previous night and had neither coat nor blanket could get one or the other by applying at the *Kammer*.

At the *Kammer* or store room I chose a great coat as I could see that if these long drawn-out roll calls continued all winter I would need one.

At seven in the evening we were again lined up for roll-call, after which each man was given a small piece of bread sent into the prison for us by the civilian population of the town. This bread was of the American Relief rations sent to the occupied areas from America by way of Holland.

One corner of these old barracks was fenced off and guarded separately from the rest, the inmates being a score or so of men who had been captured the previous November. These men wore black uniforms with brown bands around their arms. Their clothes were supplied from England, and everything else they required such as food, soap, books, cigarettes, etc. was sent from the Red Cross. All food which they did not need they passed through the wire to us. There was no doubt that their German rations were also turned back to supplement what we got.

It was comical, yet pathetic, how we poor beggars hung around that wire, for all the world like a bunch of hungry hound pups outside a kitchen door. If one managed to click a crust, the others would crowd around trying to beg a bit more from the generous donor, and if that failed, would try to beg a bite from the lucky one. If one of the black uniforms appeared smoking a cigarette, as many as half a dozen would try for the butt.

One morning, volunteers were called to go on a

working party up into the town. This was not such a joke as it would have been on the British side of the line, for of course a volunteer working party back there would have been the flattest kind of a wash-out. Things were different here, as I soon learned.

The chap on the next flop tipped me off to get on it if I could, as there was always the chance of getting a turnip or perhaps a few raw potatoes smuggled to one by some kindly French woman. He himself, the last time he was out, had managed to collect his pock-ets full of vegetables of various sorts. That being the case, I volunteered.

For five days I laboured with this party fitting up a new prison. At the end of the time I felt so weak from hunger I paraded sick. The only chance of get-ting any hand-outs was when we were either going to work or coming back at night. The gang got so they would break ranks and almost mob any person they thought looked promising. Of course this would not do. So the guards kept a tight hand on us, and the odd scraps were few and far between. But in spite of that my five days were not wholly wasted.

The man in charge of the party, a fat old Landstrummer who sported a heavy black beard, a hawk nose and a fierce expression soon discovered that I had a working knowledge of tools. After the first half day he promoted me to the position of straw-boss over a small gang erecting a partition in the new lager.

By the look of it, the building we were making over had been a brewery, but it had been burnt or bombed and was now very much out of action. I was working on a partition to wall off a part of the building too badly smashed to be worth fixing.

At a strategic point four guards stood about with rifles and fixed bayonets keeping an eye on us. It did not take me long to discover that while Blackbeard was a good carpenter he was a poor man on this par-ticular job. Windows that should have been bricked up with a mixture of cement were put in place with

51

lime mortar. The gates and fences were eight feet high instead of twelve.

The only thing for which I might have been censured was the fact that when one afternoon we ran short of six inch spikes, I finished the job with fours. The following morning when the supply of big nails was replenished, I meekly did whatever I was told to do instead of demanding to be allowed to drive some more spikes in that corner. This was important later.

The weather turned cold and miserable. In the long alley at the rear of the vacant horse stalls where we paraded for roll-call, thin mud splashed at every footfall. A drizzle of rain fell almost constantly.

Many of us had dysentery, and I soon caught it myself. The latrines were constantly filled, and a long line-up stood waiting. When a man reached a seat he was disinclined to give it up as he knew he would need it again shortly.

Pale-faced and haggard they sat in a row like ghastly crows on a rail, their bodies wrung and tortured. Unshaven, unwashed, lousy, long-haired, totally careless of their appearance, conscious only of their misery and pain. When they were importuned to leave their seats, they immediately took their places at the end of the line hoping that they could hold themselves until their turn came again. Often they could not with results that may just as easily be imagined as described.

Every morning at eight o'clock an increasing number paraded sick from dysentery and flu. The worst cases were taken to the hospital. Some of these eventually returned, but a steadily augmenting percentage failed to do so. We assumed they had died.

One night during a heavy rain seven officers broke out. They were imprisoned in a section apart from us. The guard saw the last man and captured him but the others got away for a time. In a day or two they were all brought back. The only man who ever got clear away from this prison-camp and across to our lines was an airman who worked the trick by stealing a German plane

High bulwarks circled the town. All entrances were guarded. A canal running by the western outskirts increased the hazards, and sentries were posted on every bridge. Moreover the town swarmed with German soldiery so that after sizing up the situation I did not feel in any particular hurry to try the stunt myself, especially as there were rumours that most of us were soon to be moved to the lager at Fresnes.

One day four hundred of us were moved to Fresnes into the new compound, and when the excitement of moving had died down, incredible though it may seem, the fact remained that my bed was in the same corner where I had run short of six-inch spikes!

Chapter Five

The camp sergeant was a slightly under-sized edition of a typical Prussian *unter-offizier.* Blonde hair clipped short, waxed mustache à la Kaiser, backbone like a ram-rod and a temper and vocabulary that would fuse wire. Fortunately for our collective self-respect we could understand little of what he said.

The commandant, referred to by his little charges as Hindenburg, though I believe his name was Schmidt, might have been the original of the German officer of the Allied newspaper cartoons. Standing a full six feet in height, bulky almost to fatness, close-cropped fair hair, piggish eyes, coarse nose and mouth and a triple chin, he looked a typical enemy villain in whose power any beauteous young heroine would be certain to meet "a fate worse than death."

He had power of life and death over us and over his sentries. Woe betide the guard who came under his displeasure. "Back to the trenches!" he'd roar. And how he could roar! When he got well started, those of us who didn't feel a crinkling in the short hairs on the back of his neck, experienced an almost irresistible impulse to roll over with all four paws in the air.

The real power in the camp was the interpreter, Cohen. He was a queer little duck with a decided Jewish look about him, hooked beak and sallow complexion, but he spoke German like a native. He wore the uniform of a private in a London Scottish battalion but was believed to be a German Jew. Most of us thought he was a spy, but I discounted this if only because none of us knew anything that was worth a spy's time to find out. Besides, as a spy, he was too obvious.

Cohen had lots of patience and no small amount of authority in spite of the lack of any badge of office. Often the sergeant became so incensed at us that after a broadside of vitriolic *Deutsch* he'd look as if he were about to burst with rage. The fact that we could not properly understand and appreciate the exact quality of the insults he was pouring upon us seemed by its very futility to exasperate him the more and he often threw up his hands in hopeless disgust at everything and turned the situation over to Cohen. The little Jew, with a faintly contemptuous grin, would then turn to us.

"Hah, then, you fellows," he'd begin, "Get yourselves lined up in sevens. No more or no less and for God's sake stay there until every head man has been given the loaf for his seven. You will then get the word to break away when you can divide your rations. . . All ready . . . ? Parade, SHUN!" And every little Tommee stood as straight and as still as he happened to feel like at the moment. But we kept a fair amount of order, and Cohen and Wilhelm, the little white-haired camp cook, would then carry the huge basket of brown bread down the long lines of sevens giving each front man his loaf.

I rather liked Cohen, although, since he was a member of the camp staff and bunked down along with the clerk, the mailman, the carpenter and the stretcher-bearers in a separate building, I did not get a chance to become really acquainted with him. He was placed in a difficult position - in authority yet without official recognition or badge of office - and he acquitted himself well.

One evening he appeared with a list of occupations for which volunteers were called. Bricklayers, carpenters and textile workers were in good demand. No farmers were required, but they needed threshermen. I did not at that time know much about the job but having a fair idea of the principle of threshing I gave him my name for that, figuring that if I made a bad fizzle of it I could claim the German machines were different from the ones I used to work. I was sorry the moment after they had my name as the next trade called was that of lumberman. This would have suited me exactly, and besides all the other overseas men immediately signed on for that in a body. As it eventually turned out, however, it didn't matter.

Up to this time I had been thinking more and more seriously of escaping. The thought of being drafted to a salt-mine gang was a constant dread to us all. The prospects of a decent job under better living conditions knocked a lot of zip from my notions of making a get-away. The risk seemed hardly worth while, especially as many of us expected the war to be over by Christmas. I decided to stick it out.

The dysentery now broke out worse than ever. We all swarmed with lice, and many of us looked as if we had not washed for weeks. In fact I honestly believe that fully half of our number did not wash from one week's end to another. No doubt the lack of soap contributed to that condition, though I noticed that those who so desired could keep themselves looking fairly decent. Someone had given me a piece of soap which he had begged from a French woman. It was poor stuff being made apparently of sand, wood ashes and very little fat. It was impossible to produce anything even remotely resembling lather but it helped a lot if only to one's self-respect.

Every morning after roll-call and while I was still warmed from my scalding hot drink of "tea" or "coffee" made fresh from scorched barley, I would repair to the wash-house, get washed and then go after my shirt. This was a job that took some fortitude as the wash-house was open on three sides, and the wind always seemed to blow cold.

All the big lice scouts and skirmishers that had struggled over me during the night were picked off at this time. The smaller and home-grown products were hunted during the afternoon when the air was perhaps a little warmer - thus allowing one to take off more clothes with less physical anguish. It was quite impossible to make a thorough job. The best one could do was keep them down.

Some, too lazy or careless to bother hunting lice, fairly crawled with them. Standing behind these fellows at roll-call or bread-line one could see the lice swarming in clusters on the outside of their tunics. All around their collars and even the seams down their backs were encrusted with the insects. Sometimes one of these filthy wretches managed to get the loaf at the head of his bread-line seven. Tucking it lovingly under his arm and steering for the nearest step or ledge he then proceeded to cut it up with any old knife-blade that could be procured.

More often than not the cutter-up grabbed the biggest portion leaving the smaller and weaker members of the group to scramble for their share as best they could. Occasionally when the scrimmage had disintegrated, a weakling or stand-offish chap usually found himself breadless.

At first being rather fussy, I used to peel my ration after one of these walking hostelries had had the handling of the grub. Later, I struck a better racket. I bought a knife and tried to manage it so that I got the loaf.

If I failed in that, I was usually the only one in the seven who had a knife, and it did not take a great deal of argument to get the other to hand the loaf over. Then, after the step had been carefully dusted off with my cap, I went to work. No one was allowed to touch an issue until the whole loaf was cut up and the portions evened. I then made the beggars line up and advance on the bread-pile, one at a time, leaving the last piece for me just to show the game was on the square. You may bet that when the cutter-up got the end issue he took mighty good care to cut the portions evenly.

It wasn't very long until I had worked up quite a reputation as a bread-cutter, and quite often if I had not clicked the loaf, someone would say, "Let's get the knife-man to cut it up."

One day a couple of tubs of stew were sent in from the other camp. At first we all lined up in fours, but when Cohen called for working parties to come to the front, all the late comers at the end of the parade crowded forward and tried to squeeze in close to the tubs. While the mob surged about, and before order could be restored, some had boldly dipped in their tins and made off with their booty.

The little Jew shouted and cursed and pleaded with them to go easy, and all would get some, as there was an extra quantity that day. In vain! The pressure of the crowd increased, and although he strove manfully to fight them off, even striking several with his dipper, he could not stop the rush and finally gave up and fought his way out of the scrimmage.

As soon as the last faint remnant of authority was gone, the crowd was on the tubs like a herd of ravenous hogs, upsetting the barrels immediately and fighting to dig their mess-tins into the mixture of mud and food that instantly formed beneath their feet.

I happened to be near one of the German guards who had escorted the soup into the camp, and as he watched the show, I heard him mutter to himself, "*Schwein! Schwein!*" By Gad, Fritz, I thought, for once you aren't far wrong.

That night we received no bread ration and had to make do with a mess of boiled turnip leaves. These were fearfully salt and many of the men could not eat them, though I managed to get mine down.

Afterwards, instead of turning in with the others I hung around outside waiting for one of the guards who had promised to bring me a whole loaf - for five marks. I had just given him up and was making my way to my mattress when a shot rang out.

I went back to the doorway from where I could see a dim form lying beside the north gate. I approached cautiously followed by two Imperial sergeants, as we did not know what to expect.

Bending over I recognized the wounded man as Sergeant Elmer Strate. He told us he was trying to escape by climbing over the gate, when a sentry had suddenly appeared from behind the outside wall. The German had shouted, and Strate was climbing back when the other ran up and placing his rifle against Strate's thigh shot him down.

With some difficulty we carried him into a vacant room where, in lieu of bed or stretcher, we had to lay him on the stone floor. Quickly begging some field dressings from the other prisoners we dressed the wound by the light of a candle which Cohen had brought in. From the widening pool of blood in which he lay arose a heavy-scented steam.

The shot had torn a hole that a rat could run through, the bone being smashed to splinters. In spite of our best efforts with bandages and a tourniquet, he was bleeding to death. As he felt himself grow weaker he realized this and told me, while I pillowed his head and gave him sips of water, that he was done for.

After about an hour a German doctor and his orderly came. They bound up the wound a little better and gave him a couple of morphine tablets, as he was in great pain. A little later he was taken away to the hospital in an open cart. Next morning Cohen announced that the sergeant had died during the night.

This tragic event put a damper on plans of escape which I was again considering, although there was no doubt in my mind that poor Strate had made several bad mistakes when he made his attempt. In the first place he had evidently overlooked or forgotten the fact that no matter how dark the night an object above the skyline is visible to a person standing on the ground. And this particular night was still only late evening, clear and star-lit.

One thing I learned by Strate's unfortunate attempt was the importance of so planning the actual getaway that the chances of being shot at that moment were reduced as much as possible.

By this time I was making a few acquaintances, rather against my will for the most part, as it seemed no sooner did I become friends with someone than I lost him suddenly and tragically. I knew nearly all of the overseas men by name but went out of my way to cultivate a couple of older prisoners - older both in years and prison experience - who had already made three unsuccessful attempts to escape.

These two Imperials held themselves somewhat aloof from the common herd, ganging only with one or two others who had also at one time or another tried to get away. They had the attitude of a group of matrons who have weathered successfully the vicissitudes of marriage and child-bearing; to them the chatter of mere flappers seems pointless. When once started, and, under the stimulus of a cigarette or two, they could spin escape yarns by the hour, the meat of their experiences being that a bold face often gets one through tight places.

But the shooting of Sergeant Strate cooled my enthusiasm for escape plans for several days. Then one morning the news spread that the one and only Yankee the camp could boast of had left by way of the roof during the night.

This Yank was a slim blonde from a place he called "Noo Yoik." A quaint fish in many ways, very much given to poker. He had evidently climbed up the wall inside, removed some of the tiles and jumped to the ground outside the lager. During the day we heard that the camp Commandant had paraded all the guards and given them what they were expecting. He told them that if they let one more man get away, back to the trenches they would have to go, the whole bunch of them.

Just before dark the same night a large notice appeared on the wall over-looking the alley where we paraded for roll-call. After the usual preliminary guff about "Extract from Army Orders by General Whatsit in the Field" the notice went on to inform us in very ragged English that sentries guarding prisoners were not compelled to challenge anyone attempting to escape and had orders to fire at once.

The next day another barrel of soup came up from the other camp. Again the crowd broke ranks and mobbed the man serving it out, but this time the tub did not upset.

I suppose I could have got some if I had dived in but I preferred to stand back. Many of the younger Imperials - the kids of sixteen or seventeen - also kept out of the scrimmage. All the scrambling was being done by the burly full-grown ruffians. One fellow who wore a round yellow scull cap was having a glorious time - he was in the forefront the previous day, too. I watched him actually clambering over the other's backs until he got to the tub where he dropped to the ground, feet first, I was sorry to observe. If he had fallen sideways or head first he would have been pounded to a justifiable jelly in a moment.

But he got his mess-tin full and fought his way out. On the way some of it spilled out but he still had a fair share when he broke free. And how he did fling that soup into himself! Huge mouthfuls bolted and gulped down while he kept one eye on the crowd that still milled around the tub. He knew that while they still scrambled, there was still soup, and in much less time than it takes to tell he had wolfed down the last mouthful and plunged in again, gulping as he went.

This was too much for me and I dived in after him.

Grabbing him by his greasy coat-collar I yanked him back to the plaudits of the smaller Imperials who had also been watching him. He spluttered a bit, and I thought for a minute I was going to have a fight on my hands, but he wasn't that kind of a rooster, which suited me just as well.

As I went to my thin shaving-filled mattress that night I was very hungry indeed. The only thing to supplement my meagre bread-ration was a spoonful of unsweetened cocoa powder for which I had traded a book. This I had carefully saved until I felt I could not get much hungrier.

During the afternoon I had spoken to two of our guards about bread, and they had promised to bring some in the morning if they could. But in the meantime I was ravenous and the only thing to do about it was to go to sleep and dream myself a good meal.

One who has never been really hungry for long spells cannot imagine the gorgeous banquets at which the dreamer is the star performer. Glittering glassware; gleaming white tablecloths; soft, dreamy music and food. FOOD! FOOD!

Heaps of it! Piles of it! Course after course! Roast beef surrounded by smoking brown baked potatoes. Roast pork, its rich crust scored, swimming in lakes of fat gravy. And how you eat! Helping after helping, dish after dish you clean up. The supply is never-ending nor is your appetite impaired!

One small cloud appears to mar your paradise caused by a pain in either your hip-bone or your shoulder or perhaps both. But you ignore a little thing like that and fall to with renewed gusto.

Puddings and pies! Rich cream pies; lemon pies; apple pies three feet across and eight inches deep. Huge bowls of sugar to sprinkle over them and tall flagons of thick cream! You demolish them one after another unsurprised at your capacity. A waning appetite is incomprehensible. Never again will you be really and truly "full."

You are just starting really to enjoy yourself when

- Ouch! You simply must attend to that pain. And you roll over to ease the ache of your thinly-covered bones on their hard, cold bed and you wake up and are promptly reminded of your very real and very unhappy present circumstances.

You, with millions of other unfortunates in similar camps spread over half a world, are sentenced to an indefinite term of imprisonment and slavery for no greater crime than that of being on the opposite side from that of your captors. All those dim, shapeless heaps about you and the myriad others beyond are exiled from family, home, friends, comforts, cleanliness - everything that makes life worth while. Until the world ceases its madness, their lot is filth, disease, hunger, cold, lice, misery, imprisonment - a phase of war more authentic than the flag waving and the stirring platform speeches.

As you lie staring at the rafters, tiny visitors from the next mattress slowly creep, creep and faintly tickle as they pass over your flesh to wherever they are bound for -Ugh! You shudder and, turning, bury your face beneath the filthy blanket and woo again that wonderful dream paradise.

The moment you fall asleep, there it is once more. The festal board, all the food in the world to eat and you the only one with appetite enough to handle the job!

The hoped-for extra bread failed to turn up the following morning. The guards said it was very hard to get and although they promised to try again they held out little hope. I asked the British corporal who worked in the cook-house how the chances were for a "buckshee loaf." He said he would see what he could do and would let me know later. Satisfied I had pulled all the strings pullable and if a loaf was for sale in the camp it would come my way, I went back to my mattress and tried to go to sleep again.

Chapter Six

I had not been lying there long before a young Imperial from a London regiment came and set himself beside me. After a few careful glances about he asked cautiously, "J'ever fink of miking a brike for it?" I looked at the youngster in surprise. He was a scrawny runt if ever I saw one. He appeared to be about seventeen years old, though being London bred he might have been twenty. He was thin and he was dirty. His hair hung in filthy wisps and clots over his coat collar. His face had not known a razor for months and the sparse fungoid growth seemed to sprout from the dirt on his cheeks. He had been sick with dysentery, as I had often bought his bread ration for a mark a time when he was too sick to eat it himself. He spent the money on the kickless German cigarettes.

As a partner I felt certain he would be a rotten investment. But to see what he would say more than anything, I answered carelessly, "Oh, sure! I'll probably take a crack at it one of these days."

"When yeh gow will yer tike me along wiv yer? Will yer?" he whined, his poor, weak-looking face with its scrubby beard quite lit up by the eagerness in his eyes as he pleaded.

I could have kicked myself for giving the poor little beggar any encouragement. To remedy my foolishness I replied, "Aw, shucks, now, Kid. You could never stand the gaff of an escape. You might be out a week or more before getting across the lines. How would you get along for grub? You get no seventh of a loaf twice a day on that game, you know."

"I don't eat much. A turnip or two would do me."

"True, you don't eat much, But that's because you've been sick. How far do you think you could run if you were chased by a couple of Heinies with a vision of ten days' leave if they caught you?"

"As near as I can figure it out," I went on, "there's only one chance in a hundred of a man getting across at his first attempt. Perhaps one in twenty at his second go and one in ten from then on. Remember this, too, if you get caught old Hindenburg will make it plenty hot for you with pack drill, short rations, solitary confinement and perhaps a few other things."

He nodded. "Yes, I've thought of all that but I still fink I could stick it."

I grunted impatiently. "Huh! You think you could while you're sitting there. It's so long since you were on a march, you've forgotten what it feels like to be all in and have to keep going."

"However," I went on more kindly, "you think it over. I may tip you off to something one of these days."

When he had gone I lay back again and did a bit of thinking myself. No word had been received about the jobs for which we had given our names. Certainly by this time my thresherman job was a washout as harvest was pretty well over. The cold, wet weather made winter seem close at hand and the thought of spending its long, cold, dreary months in that filthy barn of a place gave me the horrors.

If we were not kept at Fresnes then we would likely be sent to some working camp in Germany. Then, if the war kept on, as it seemed to have the habit of doing, that would mean a long walk home from there. Besides, the difficulties would be enhanced by the fact that every soul encountered in Germany would be an enemy. To get away from this camp would be much easier than from an old-established prison where all the weak spots would have been reinforced or extra-guarded long ago.

Of course our men were advancing, or so the rumours were, and a lot of the fellows were chanting the old refrain about the war being over by Christmas. But that was a very old story to me, and hope deferred had made me pretty hard-boiled.

Sure, we were advancing. We had advanced before, in the Somme, at Passchendaele in the teeth of those murderous pillboxes, over the hill at Vimy and a full dozen other places, and after a time the advance had petered out, and we had sat down until it was Fritz's turn to advance.

The long weeks and months and years had ground by, but the war was still on and apparently was good for another year or two yet. Only a few months ago the enemy was hiking for Paris faster than the French could get out of his way. Did not our Commander back at Corps Headquarters, to stiffen our panicky spines, issue his famous declarations: "Your mothers will never miss you," and "You will advance or fall where you stand facing the enemy . . ." How bitterly we laughed at that heroic slush!

This enemy who could so put our wind up such a short time ago could do it again when his turn came. No, it was of little use telling me the war would soon be over. I had heard that yarn before.

On the other hand, my skin, though dirty and tight-drawn over my ribs was yet whole; no small thing to be thankful for after three years of fighting. Our guards were evidently bent on holding down their bomb-proof jobs, if vigilance could do it. To try an escape just yet would be decidedly risky; on the other hand there was a strong rumour afloat that a large draft were being sent to the salt-mines in the near future, and I certainly wanted to dodge that parade if I could.

Another thing, I had dysentery and it was getting worse. A particularly virulent type of influenza was also raging in the camp. It seemed to me that if I was ever going to have a try for it, the sooner I started the better. Thus I weighed the matter, pro and con, and at the end of the debate the ayes had it by a big majority.

It was decided. I arose and hied me forth to seek the camp carpenter. From him I begged a piece of iron about a foot and a half long. He was an Imperial, captured the previous March at Cambrai and a chubby, good-natured sort.

"What you going to do with it?" he asked.

"Dig out through that lumber partition on the ground floor," I told him.

"Dig out through that wooden partition?" he echoes. "You'll never do it! Since you were working on the job, the outside has been wired and cross-wired back and forth, until there's hardly a hand-space that isn't wired and stapled. I know the kind of job that was done behind that partition because I did most of it myself."

"Hmm, well, we'll see. I can have this bar anyway, huh?"

"Sure you can have it and my good wishes. I don't think you can get through, but if you should, don't forget there's a sentry outside every night at dusk."

"I'll remember. Thanks old chap."

On my way back to my mattress and the corner from where I intended to escape I met the kid. "Well," I asked him cheerfully, "and what do you think about it now?"

"Ow, jist the sime as I did before. Oi'm sure I could stick."

"All right, then, come along with me and keep watch while I dig out. I'm going tonight."

"Tonight!" he cried, pretty well taken aback.

"Yeah, c'mon and let's get busy."

He followed me to my corner without another word. Of course it was useless under the circumstances to try to keep my fellow prisoners from knowing what was going on, as I was under the observation of at least a hundred men whenever they cared to look my way.

With my bar then for a pry, I went to work on the partition where I knew it to be weak. As I expected, I had no great difficulty working the boards loose, but they made a terrible racket as the bar loosened the nails or split the planks. Fortunately there was always quite a row going on in daytime, so the little extra noise I made went unnoticed by the sentries.

As soon as I had one plank loose I saw that what the carpenter has said about the wire on the back was perfectly true. However, once I had sprung one plank out far enough to get my hand through I was able to use my spoon on the staples which were short and came out with little difficulty. Working as I was doing at the end of the partition where it joined the brick wall my job was simply to loosen a couple of planks, extract the staples where the turn of the wire was made, bend the wire back into place and readjust the planks so that they looked to a casual passerby as if they had not been tampered with. That done, I left the Kid on guard for Germans in case any of them had heard the noise and came round to investigate, while I went off to attend to a little business.

My first port of call was the officers' section. Here I walked boldly in and asked to speak to an officer of the airforce if one were present. One of the number stepped forward, and I could tell by his ribbons that he had been around.

"I'd like to know, sir, just how many canals lie between here and our lines, where they are situated and any information you may have as to their depth and if they are wired below the surface."

"Oho," he chuckled, "so someone you know is going to have a try at it, eh? Well, I will tell you what I can though I can't tell you all you want to know. The only canal you must cross is the Canal de la Sensee - that is, if you want to cut across and get to the lines

69

by the shortest route. As to wiring under the surface, I have heard that has been done but I have no certain knowledge. Also I don't know anything about the depth, but you can be pretty sure of eight or ten feet. Are you a good swimmer?"

I shook my head. "I could probably make fifty yards under good conditions, but I would hesitate to do it with my clothes on and in cold water."

"Ah, that makes it bad. And if the canal is really wired you'd drown like a trapped rat." I agreed with him there but pointed out that I could perhaps find a piece of timber to help me float across and hold up my chin in case my legs caught in the wire.

"Yes," he thought that might be managed.

He then drew for me a rough map marking the chief towns along my route and the railways I had to cross. After telling me all he could, he and the other officers gathered about a dozen or so hard little Red Cross cakes and presented them to me with best wishes for my success.

I next paid a visit to the cook-house corporal who informed me that Wilhelm the head cook would sell a ration loaf for five marks. This I promptly forked over and I was soon on my way back to my corner with the spoils.

The Kid reported that no one had been snooping around so, as he had no reserve of food, I gave him half a dozen of the little cakes and told him to go and get stoked up.

While I was disposing of my few possessions to my fellow prisoners, including my precious great-coat which I thought would be too heavy, the two Imperials I have already mentioned, came around and sat on the bed.

"We hear you're going to have a try for it," said one.

"Yes," I answered. Then with a rueful grin, I added, "If my heart doesn't fail me in the meantime."

They looked the corner over and peeped through a crack across the wide, vacant part of the building I

70

had to cross, through the empty, gaping window space beyond to where the night sentry kept his watch beside the outer wall.

"What time you gonna start?" asked the other.

"Between eight and half past tonight," I told him. "Like to come along?"

"What do you think about it, Sandy?" asked the last speaker. Sandy took another look through the crack, shook a board which squealed harshly and then sat down beside his chum.

"Well," he finally announced, "I'd like to have another go, but in my opinion the first man to step through the breach would need his nerve." It would take more nerve, perhaps, to lead the way but it seemed to me the danger was less, since what noise the first one made might bring a guard to investigate in time to catch the others. I did not explain this to them as I didn't want to shatter their admiration of my bravery.

They talked it over together and finally decided to follow me out through the hole and make another attempt to reach our lines. While they were discussing the matter, I'm blessed if four others of the Kid's regiment didn't come up and also investigate the proposed exit.

"Please Teacher, can we go too?" seemed to be the question of the moment.

"Suit yourselves," I told them hospitably, "I'm going first and I sure won't wait to bung up the hole after me. For all I care you can organize a general exodus."

Taking the Kid on one side I spoke to him like a Dutch uncle. "See here now, youngster," I never did learn his name "this is a pretty risky game. It's nothing less than craziness for you to think you can make it. Take my tip and stay here out of the wet. If you go through that hole you are apt to get into the hottest mess of your life."

"Oi knaow, but Oi'm sure Oi can mike it." he insisted.

71

"Well then, I'll tell you candidly, I'd rather go alone. I think my chances of getting away are better, but if you are dead set on following me you may, so long as you keep up. If you play out, I'll leave you. On the other hand, I'm none too fit myself and I may be the one to fall out. In which case you inherit the remaining grub, if any, and are at liberty to go on if you like. I know this sounds pretty brutal and I hate to hurt your feelings but the fact remains that I'm not a tom-cat and have only one life to risk. If having you along this time means I'm recaptured, I may get shot next time."

He begged and pleaded with me to let him come, and after much argument and insistence that he would not be a hindrance I finally consented though very much against my judgement.

Dusk fell between half past eight and nine o'clock. To post a sentry outside the north wall at eight was too early if he was on only during the night. Nine o'clock saw it pretty murky, and he would or should be on hand before that time. From what I knew of guard duties in the army, it is very unusual to post a man at any other time than on the hour. But this was a special post, and it was quite likely he went on at the half hour, almost certainly not at quarter past. So, then, I figured his nibs would come on duty at half past eight. And the darkest and safest possible minute for the attempt would be quarter past eight. Eight-fifteen would be the hour!

Immediately after roll-call, the Kid and I went straight to my corner, where we sat down together and waited.

Everything was ready. I had washed my feet and put on a clean pair of socks as I knew what a difference that made on a long tramp. My loaf was cut up and distributed among my several pockets as were also the Red Cross biscuits. I tried to eat the ration of bread I had just received but my mouth was too dry and I couldn't get it down. The Kid was in like case. He sat there with his chunk in his hands nibbling nervously at the corner.

"Better put it in your pocket," I suggested. "If you aren't hungry now you will be."

The crowd had all come back into the huge hall. They were getting their beds straightened up for the night while there was still a little light. Under cover of the noise they were making we would get out.

Presently along came the other six who also proposed to follow me. A man of the Royal Canadian Regiment to whom I had bequeathed my overcoat was the official time keeper, since he was the only one in camp I knew who had a watch. The minutes crawled while we sat or stood about, saying little, our faces pale and drawn.

"Five minutes yet." proclaimed the timekeeper in answer to a tense question.

My nerves were edgy, I noticed, and I hoped they would continue so. Had I forgotten anything? Was there any factor that would mitigate against our success that I had overlooked? I mentally scanned the layout but could detect no flaw in the plans. I knew exactly what I would do if I were seen. A bold front - the explanation that I was on fatigue - anything of that sort to get me past the danger moment. If I did encounter a German I certainly figured on seeing him first.

"Eight-fifteen!"

I arose. "Well, goodbye, old brass polisher. Be good to my little pets in that coat. Think of me in the Corner House ten days from now." We shook hands.

To the Kid I looked the question he was expecting. "Oi'm ready, lead on," he answered. The plucky little beggar! I did not think he would have the nerve when it came to the last moment, and in admiration for his grit I gripped his hand. "Good egg," I whispered. "Come on, then!"

In a few moments I had the hole ready and then I turned to repeat my last instructions. He was not to follow until I crossed the floor of the vacant portion of the building and was through the open window space. If all was clear I would then wave to him. He nodded to show he understood, and I scrambled through the breach and down on to the concrete floor. I was out!

The moment my hob-nailed boots touched that concrete I knew I would have to take them off before I dare go a step farther. The little bit of loose grit on the surface made a noise under my footfall that fairly screamed in that empty vault.

Quickly telling the Kid to get some one else to take off his boots for him while he kept watch for me, I tore at my laces. The time seemed an age, while I crouched clawing at the knots, yet it was probably only a few seconds before I was speeding silently across to the window opening.

A quick glance to the right and left and I scrambled through. Turning, I gave the Kid the *All Clear* signal and with my boots in my hand dashed across the yard to the wall.

This open yard was partially under the observation of sentries. I did not dare to look around after I had started to run, but kept going my hardest, knowing well that if I were seen I would hear soon enough. Fifty yards . . . Twenty . . . Safe! I hurled myself over the wall and sank down behind it with a gasp of relief. While waiting for the Kid to come out I put on my boots. In a moment or two he had joined me and before he had got his boots on again, three others of the Kid's mob in quick succession had joined us.

"Where are the others?" I asked in a whisper when no more appeared.

"They said it was too light yet," answered the last comer.

"All right, then, that lets me out fine. As soon as you fellows get your boots on, follow us on farther into this garden to more cover and wait. While it gets dark we'll talk over what to do next."

My plan was to lie doggo here until it got quite dark before striking out in earnest. But as I waited for the others to come down to us I noticed the moon for the first time, about nine days old, clear and not likely to set for another two hours or more. To forget about such a thing as moonlight on a game like this was a serious error indeed. I wanted utter darkness, of course, but to lay hid for half of every night waiting for that would so delay us that we might be starved into giving ourselves up. There was no help for that now. We were out, and I for one intended to stay out as long as possible.

Soon, one by one, the others crawled down and lay beside us in the shelter of some turnips whose wide tops nearly covered us. Sitting up then, in a whisper I demanded to know what these other three had planned. There was silence for a little, then one, a corporal, answered, "Well, we were thinking it would be safer for us all to keep together, so that in case we met several Germans we could put up a scrap for it.

"Hunh," I snorted, "that's all very well, but if we did that and happened to kill or even wound one of them we could expect a mighty quick finish if we were nabbed later on. You've got to remember we've a canal to cross and every bridge on it will be guarded. They may also have wired the canal bed so that it will be impossible to swim. The little bit of risk you have taken will be nothing to what you have at the Canal and later at the firing line."

"We heard once," he returned, "of a party of four that got through all right, and they said they got along much better than they could have done alone or in pairs. Besides," he pointed out, "there is that Canal to cross anyway, and perhaps a bunch of us could sneak up and overpower the sentry."

I had already thought of this but I had pretty well discarded the plan.

"No!" I stated flatly, "If I can't get out of this mess without scragging some poor dub who thinks he's got a bomb-proof job on bridge-guard, I'll let myself be recaptured and go back and take my medicine. Them's my sentiments."

"But we don't need to kill him," argued the corpo-

75

ral, "we could just . . ."

"Oh, rats!" I interrupted. "While you were being careful not to kill him and at the same time keep him from making a noise, the rest of his pals would be certain to hear the scuffle and turn out to lend a hand. Whether we got across the bridge or not, the whole German army would be out hunting for us. "No," I concluded, "we get through by stealth or not at all. Force is strictly out for me."

"Well, anyway," he said gloomily, "if we don't go with you we might as well give ourselves up, since we know nothing of night travelling. You're a prairie man and know all about that sort of thing."

"All right then," I replied. "You fellows can come, but I want you all to bear in mind that I am the undisputed little cock of this little walk. Whatever I say, goes - and instantly. Does the whole bunch understand that. Is that clear?"

"That satisfies me exactly. What do you fellows say?" The others agreed unreservedly and seemed well content.

We waited there for another half hour while I chewed turnip leaves to relieve my dry mouth. By that time it was as dark as it would get until after the moon set. Then, as I arose to my feet preparatory to leading the way westward and homeward, my ears caught the last few bars of the *Soldier's Farewell* being sung by our late comrades back in the camp. Distance softened the discords and mellowed the harmony of the voices as they rose and fell and finally died away:

Farewell, farewell, my own true love,
Farewell, farewell, my own true love.

Whenever I hear that plaintive lament, memory whips me back to that night in the turnip patch as we started off on our Great Adventure. It may be that those who knew, started the old melody as a cheering goodbye and wanted us to know they wished

76

us well. Be that as it may, the circumstances were such that I grinned to myself as I nudged the Kid to follow me at a few yards. The others were also to proceed at intervals and to go very carefully until we had got well away from the prison.

At the lower end of the garden we came to a thick-set hedge at the top of a railway embankment. Down below and immediately in front of us we could hear voices and the noise of men walking about on the railway. To our left a signal cabin threw a strong light almost up to the prison camp, and on the right a short distance lay the straggling village of Fresnes. We seemed to be stuck already.

After a little cautious craning about in order to size up the situation I turned to the right, following the hedge along for a hundred yards or so which took us as close to the village as I deemed advisable. No one was on the railway just here, but we could see those we had recently avoided. I paused at a gap until the others had crept up to me. "Keep close up," I muttered and wiggled through the gap and slid down the bank. The four others followed making what seemed like a tremendous row. At the bottom I led the way, walking boldly across the scrunching cinders followed closely by the others.

The bluff worked. The Germans to the left paid no attention as the light was not strong enough for them to see our uniforms. They probably took us for a small working party on legitimate business.

Once across the railway we emerged into open fields across which we could see for two or three hundred yards quite plainly. Here we quickened our pace and walked with less caution. I paused long enough, however, to impress upon the others that because I was in the lead they were not to depend on me to do all the watching. The danger of meeting someone was so acute that every eye was needed.

We had been following a faint path which led due west when I suddenly noticed three Germans coming along another path at an angle which would cut ours and cause them to meet us when our paths crossed. In my dismay to see them so close I checked my pace during which moment the others looked up and caught sight of them too.

Without a word I started off again at an angle to the left of our previous course and walking as quickly as possible without actually drawing attention to ourselves by an unwonted speed. One man broke into a run but just as he went to pass me I grabbed him and pulled him back.

For a few moments the situation looked bad as the Germans drew closer. Then as they passed behind us about fifteen yards distant, we all breathed a lot easier.

Soon we came to more wooded country through which ran ditches partially filled with water. This I did not discover until bursting through a tangle of brambles I fell splash into one. In an instant I was wet through up to my thighs but I had learned my lesson and from there on we travelled more circumspectly. I also chose myself a good stout stick which came in very useful for testing the depth of water in the ditches.

The country through which we travelled grew more and more heavily wooded until we were among heavy timber. In places this had been cut down leaving a bad tangle of slashed-off branches. Through these slashings the bracken and brambles had grown to a height of four feet.

After about two hours of steady going we halted for a brief rest in an open glade. As the others had brought no food whatever, I divided among them my few remaining cakes and part of my bread. When we had eaten, and the corporal had bummed a couple of blank leaves from my diary with which to make some beech-leaf cigarettes, we continued on our way.

For miles I forced a passage through dew-drenched undergrowth keeping the North Star a little past my right shoulder.

Once we came out upon an old logging road leading roughly in the right direction and along this we followed for half a mile or more until I espied two objects standing in the road some little distance ahead. They might only have been tall stumps but as we stared at them, they seemed to move, so I left the road and made a wide detour.

Every now and then we heard a weird howling whistle. It would rise, hold its note for half a minute, then die down. Presently, off it would go again.

The corporal gave it as his opinion that our escape had been discovered, and the whistle was to appraise everyone to keep a lookout for us. Later, I learned that we were unduly disturbed over that noise, as it was blown when our aircraft were expected.

These woods, known as the Forest de Raismes, covered a large area. In pre-war days there must have been some valuable timber here but the Germans had worked the forest until there was nothing left but vast expanses of slashings and bracken with only odd patches of inferior stuff left standing. We turned to the right following a cinder path which ran beside the railway. Suddenly I saw the outline of a locomotive engine loom up before us.

I stopped short, certain there would be a guard somewhere about but doubtful if he heard us. My doubts were soon dispelled. A foot stirred in the cinders ahead and a sharp "*Wer da?*" barked out.

Dead silence for a moment. Again came the challenge.

"Come on," I whispered, "follow on and perhaps we can bluff him into thinking we are a working party who haven't heard his challenge."

I stepped boldly out of the shelter of the bushes and started to walk over the metals. We were unfortunately placed as we were between the sentry and the moon which was by now almost setting. We were visible to him while he remained invisible to us.

I was almost over and was restraining an impulse to dash for the shelter of the woods when he fired, the bullet striking the twigs over my head. Without a word we all dived for the shrubbery, scattering like a flock of frightened partridges.

Another shot also high up. As we dashed through the undergrowth I chuckled to myself with the thought that he was making the usual mistake of aiming too high at night. Then he fired again. This time immediately behind me I heard a slight crash followed by a thud on the ground. I stopped, came back and looked down. It was the Kid!

Chapter Seven

I couldn't believe it at first. The others had scattered in all directions, as I could tell by the sound of their going, but he had clung to my heels. Only a moment before he had been following me, eager and confident that soon he would be safe home in England and now he lay at my feet quivering, his boots making a little rustle in the leaves. The bullet had gone through his head entering just above the right ear and coming out through the left temple.

Suddenly a flood of hot, bitter rage welled up in me, and I started back toward the sentry who was still firing. Behind me pandemonium had broken loose. From the buildings I could hear the inmates tumbling out and shouting questions to the sentry. With rifles, revolvers and lanterns they spread out and started to search the scrub firing as they advanced.

A bullet which zipped close by me and smacked into a poplar nearby brought me to my senses. Of course it was only the fortune of war. The sentry had challenged twice and to fire was only his duty. Certainly I would not help my own case by madly charging a man with a loaded gun. The fortune of war! I was soldier enough to appreciate that, so I turned, and protecting my face with my bowed outstretched arms, I raced away from my pursuers as hard as I could go.

When the pursuit was shaken off I stopped in the deep shadow of a spruce. I could hear rustlings and twigs snapping all around me but did not know whether they were friend or foe so did not care to call or whistle. I must have waited there for nearly half an hour during which time the noises died away, and the voices had apparently returned to their camp. Then, realizing it was useless to wait longer, I started off again.

After another few miles of terrifically heavy going through waist-high slashings, I came out on a road which, however, swung too far to the south for my liking. But it was much easier walking, and I followed it for a time while I rested somewhat after the exertions of forcing my way through the bush.

About two in the morning as near as I could judge, I emerged from the forest into a long sloping field that led down to what looked to be a canal. A fairly large town which later proved to be St. Amand was visible upon its banks. I approached the canal very cautiously and with much difficulty, too, as there were a number of deep drainage ditches hereabout that were a great trial.

At the canal I looked to right and left but could see no boat or timber of any kind that would help me across so I followed the canal south toward the town in the hope of coming across something. Nothing was discovered, and I presently found myself well down into the town. Just ahead was the main traffic bridge, limbers and motor lorries continually rattling over it.

Leaving the canal bank I crossed several gardens and after climbing two or three backyard fences came out on the main road. It was my intention to wait in the shadow until a party of men or a number of vehicles came along from the east when I would fall in behind them and hope to pass as a connecting file or brakesman to a wagon and thus get by the sentry and over the bridge. But my luck was out - all the traffic was coming from the wrong direction.

I waited for quite a time, then as all traffic of any sort appeared to have ceased for the night, I decided to get out of the town, make a wide circle to the southward and see how the canal looked down there. With this idea in mind I turned up the street and stole quietly along. Suddenly I heard a slight sound just ahead as if someone had moved his foot.

I froze instantly. Then it flashed across me that as I came down into the town there looked to be the grounds of a chateau on my left. In that case the main entrance would be up this way somewhere. Chateaux are usually occupied by general staffs so the step I heard would be that of the sentry at the gate. As quickly and as quietly as possible I turned and edged backward when I heard, closer this time, a distinct, though very cautious footfall. He was stalking me.

Before me now was the canal bridge, strongly guarded of course. The only way of escape was back the way I had come. I had just climbed over the wall that ran by the roadside when my pursuer, discarding caution, ran up and paused by the wall, evidently wondering which way I had gone. Without waiting to see if he could follow me over I took to my heels as hard as I could go, making my way back to the canal, across the ditches and out into the open fields. When I was satisfied that I had shaken him off I travelled south for several miles before again turning westward.

Soon the fields gave way to heavy wooded country, and after I had walked for another two hours straight west without coming upon the canal I decided it was not the one I had to cross.

About dawn the forest began to open up into park lands. It was then time to hunt for cover for the day. On taking to the heavier woods once more I presently spied a thick clump of bushes almost surrounded by a bad tangle of slashings and bracken. Here I decided to lay up but I noticed as I walked through the bracken that I left a plainly marked trail so I backed in, straightening the bent fronds at every step to cover my tracks.

Gaining the heart of my little clump I sat down and removed my shoes and wrung out my socks. I was soaked to the waist and so I took off my pants and did the same to them. Then, after eating a little bread and writing my diary up to date I tried to get some sleep.

Shortly after daybreak I heard voices approaching. Nearer and nearer they came, apparently headed straight for my hiding place. They went on, however, just the other side of my clump. I wondered how it was that anyone would be passing through that apparently trackless under-brush without making more noise than they did.

The mystery was solved a few minutes later when I again heard voices approaching. These people were evidently pushing a small truck, and by the rumble of the vehicle, I guessed there was a light railway track immediately beyond where I lay hidden.

Anyone who knows his woodcraft is acquainted with the fact that ten feet off the side of any path or track through the woods is just as wild appearing as if it were ten miles. I knew this, of course, but had forgotten it and had omitted to "circle" my retreat before taking to cover. But it was too late to remedy the oversight then and so I had to lie perfectly still all day lest my slightest movement give me away to a passer-by.

I had often heard of men sleeping "with one eye open" but I didn't think it was possible to actually sleep and yet be so acutely sensitive to the slightest sound. Once a baby rabbit came sidling along very quietly to investigate me, and the faint rustle of the grass woke me instantly. Another time a bird fluttering overhead did it. The step of a man one hundred yards away would bring me fully awake.

Luckily it was a glorious day for once, and the sun dried my clothes so that on towards noon I really felt quite comfortable. About sundown I ate some more of my precious bread.

At dusk I again stole forth but on gaining the edge of the wood, a scant half mile further on, I found it so light that I sat down for a while and watched the dim, red glow of the sunset fade to saffron and pale blue and still later to violet.

While the twilight deepened, I hearkened to the sounds of the evening. Voices I heard, some distant and others so close I could almost hear what they said. Women's voices and that of a child. A dog barked, and some ducks quacked. Home sounds for someone, I supposed. Well, with a bit of luck during the next three days and it would not be long before sounds like that would be home to me. But in the meantime every moment carried its danger of dis-covery and recapture. Every snapping twig or rustle of leaves meant the possible approach of an enemy. I felt myself as one of the wolves and foxes and other hunted things.

In a way, I thought, it must be worse to be a hunted man than a hunted animal. The man is cursed by his imagination which conjures up a thousand situ-ations of danger and he continually mills over in his mind what he would do in this or that emergency. Then, when the crucial moment leaps at him it is always different from any he has foreseen. If the man takes to his heels the best he can do is a pitifully clumsy flounder compared to the swift dart of a wolf or rabbit.

At last I started off in earnest, though the moon was very bright and clear, and I had to proceed with the greatest caution. I was following along a faint path when I came suddenly upon an open space in which were a number of farm buildings from two of which lights were shining. Stepping cautiously I kept to the path rather than circle and perhaps make a noise in the bush. As I drew nearer I noticed that one light came from the barn and someone inside was doing something with a steady, thump, thump, thump, thump!

The sound was not regular enough to be an engine of any sort, and I could not guess what was going on in there at that time of night but being suspicious that Germans might be in occupation I stole on past without anyone, not even the dog, being any the wiser.

A little later I had to do a bit of quick thinking. I had just crossed a railway that I decided was the one that ran between Valenciennes and Douai and was following a faint path that led through a small pasture field. The field was surrounded by a high thickset hedge, and my path disappeared through a gap in it.

It was, by this time, so late and the land here so open, that I was stepping along at a good clip feeling fairly secure. Walking boldly to the gap I strode through and into the moonlight beyond and there, not fifty yards away were two Germans walking down the same path toward me!

For a moment I hesitated. If I deliberately turned around and ran back the way I came it would look suspicious and they would be likely to give chase on general principles. If I dodged back through the gap and tried to get out of the pasture somewhere else I might find myself in a trap. To continue forward was out of the question as the light was so strong they would see at once that I was an enemy.

My only hope was to hold my ground. With the moon in their faces and myself in the shadow of the hedge they would not be able to get a very good view of me until they were right up close. A bold front then might see me through.

Stepping back under the hedge I effected a quick change. Jerking my cap around so that the peak would not show and undoing the brass buttons of my tunic and tucking them in out of sight I hoped that a casual glance would give them the impression that I also was a German. As they came on, one carrying a heavy sack, I leaned forward upon my stick and made a noise that I hoped sounded like a German challenge. Evidently it didn't, for they made no answer but continued steadily toward me.

As they came up and passed through the gap within two feet of me they peered forward to see who I was. I also peered at them as if to enquire who they were and what was their business at that time of night. To my intense relief they kept right on without speaking and they had no sooner disappeared through the gap behind me than I took to my heels at top speed.

Many times that night I saw people fairly close at hand and either ran for it or hid. Once I flopped into a ditch when I had no other retreat and I heard a German hunting around and muttering to himself. He had evidently seen me and wondered why I disappeared so suddenly.

About three, occurred one of the strangest incidents of the whole adventure. In my diary I wrote of it, as it seemed to have happened. But years of solid, everyday security have passed since that night, and I am now more or less pleased to think that it was only a sort of waking dream, brought on by utter weariness and a little delirium most likely. However, I will tell of what *seemed* to happen though I do not expect anyone to believe it. In fact, I rather doubt it myself, now that time has dulled the sharp impression it made upon me.

The weather had changed for the worse. The moon had long since set, and a huge bank of clouds rising from the west obscured the stars, so that I had to keep my direction as best I could by taking bearings on tall landmarks such as church steeples, mine towers, clumps of trees and such objects that showed dimly above the skyline.

Soon it began to rain, quietly at first and then gradually increasing in vigour. For the previous hour or more I had been walking more slowly, stopping

87

frequently for short rests. About the time the rain commenced to fall in real earnest, I stumbled over a lump of dirt and fell prone, and so utterly fagged out was I that I just stretched out with my head resting on my arm. Every over-wrought nerve and muscle in my body prayed for sleep, though the thunder crashed, and the rain teemed down upon me.

A more dreary scene would be hard to imagine. I was in an open field overgrown with coarse grass. At distances of a mile or two when the lightning flashed I caught glimpses of mining villages. I seemed absolutely alone in a wet, dark and dismal world.

While I lay there I must have dozed for presently I fancied I heard music . . . and singing . . . and among other strains a thread of an old favourite that went, "The way is dark, and I am far from home." The music and the singing seemed to fade away, and I became conscious of an odour of wet khaki. Khaki that reeked of pain-wrenched sweat and warm blood that penetrated steadily through the fabric. I was brought fully awake by a hand that gripped and lifted my shoulder.

I wearily raised my head, too numb with fatigue to care who or what I should see, but no one was there. I did not feel in the least afraid, although the pressure of the hand remained and with little or no effort on my part, helped me to my feet and led me along, taking a course a little to the south of that which I had been following.

Soon I came to a small cluster of houses which I approached from the rear. Although I had up to this time avoided any building that might conceivably harbour a number of Germans I felt not the slightest fear or hesitation in this case.

At the back of one of the houses was a small shed with a door standing ajar. As I peered inside the lightning flashed showing me a small cart loaded with straw. The fodder hung down over the whiffle-tree so that anyone lying beneath the cart would be quite hidden from view. With a little effort I crawled under and sank down with a sigh of relief upon a little bed a dog had evidently used.

Outside the storm raged worse than ever, the rain simply pouring down, and while it stormed and thundered, I fell asleep as peacefully as if I had been warm and dry and in my own bed at home.

The storm was just clearing off when I awoke, and the last few raindrops were spotting as I emerged from my shelter. Feeling greatly refreshed and deeply grateful to whatever agency or state of mind had led me to that sanctuary I continued my journey.

From then until dawn I made good time. I knew I was drawing near to the line by the deserted appearance of the fields and when I started to descend a long, gentle slope towards a wide valley I guessed that my long-expected Sensee Canal was near at hand.

As the sky began to brighten I kept a sharp lookout for a likely place to hole up for the day. No trees or shelter of any kind seemed to be in sight. Parties of Germans were visible in all directions and had to be constantly dodged. Often while avoiding one lot I would almost run into another. The light was growing fast, and in desperation I finally took to cover among a few dried weeds that grew about as high as my knee.

I had had no time to circle my proposed bed, and before I had been there two minutes along rattled an ammunition wagon only a few yards away. I could tell by the noise that it was a hard road and that there would probably be traffic up and down all day but it was now too late to move. My only chance was to copy the system of the other hunted creatures and blend into the colour scheme of my surroundings.

After the wagon had passed well beyond me I started to camouflage myself. I dare not raise my head and had to keep flat on my back and it was with the very greatest difficulty I managed to loosen my boot-laces, partly to ease my feet and partly to allow the entrance of weeds and tufts of grass. All the time, too, cramps in my toes and the muscles in my legs gave me the devil but finally my shoes and legs were so well covered I could hardly find them myself!

I took out my first-aid scissors - short-bladed, round-pointed old veterans of many a bloody half hour - and snipped holes in my tunic in all directions. Through the holes I threaded more leaves; down inside my collar, overhanging my face, around my cap - every place that would support a leaf or stalk.

I looked and felt more like one of the Babes in the Wood than a soldier out to save the world from tyranny. That was by far the longest day I ever put in. The ground was saturated from the rain and bitterly cold besides, although on toward noon the sun came out and warmed me a little. Occasionally one of our batteries dropped a few biggish ones on the road beside me but except for the sound of the whizzing fragments overhead, they did not bother me greatly. I knew that unless one happened to fall directly on me, I was pretty safe. And if a shell did score a bulls-eye it wouldn't trouble me much anyway.

By the cessation of traffic after full daylight and the occasional shelling of the area I concluded that my hill was under the observation of our batteries. We probably held the other bank of the valley, and the line was somewhere in between. I dared not let myself hope that we held the canal.

Between myriad hopes and fears and the cold chill of the ground striking up through my saturated clothes to my half-famished body I endured the long day through. For hours I watched a spider weaving her web between a fern that sprouted from my right breast pocket and a withered pig weed that apparently held its rest in my left armpit. Up and down, back and across in a beautifully symmetrical pattern. And when we had our net completed and had taken a seat in the background to await results how we eyed each tiny prospective winged victim that flitted and hovered and finally lit upon every spot but the right one!

And then our ultimate joy when a tiny moth did get tangled by one wing! How we scampered over the rigging and gobbled her down! Returning later to our ring-side seat to pick our teeth with our front leg!

After what seemed a minor eternity, the sun did set, and at the earliest possible moment I left my weedy bed and started off again. I judged I was not more than two miles from the line and possibly not one mile. I resolved to proceed with the very greatest caution. If it took me three days to get through I was not going to spoil my chances by trying to rush things.

"Careful does it," was the motto.

After avoiding several small parties of Germans I continued cautiously, stealing yard by yard nearer the wooded valley. Once I nearly stumbled upon a battery of field-guns. The gunners looked up when I suddenly appeared but I instantly changed direction and kept on walking past paying them no attention. They said nothing, the distance being too great for them to notice the colour of my uniform. I proceeded even more carefully from then on, and at last, climbing a low bank fringed with willows I discovered myself upon the brink of the canal.

I looked cautiously in both directions but could see no one. Neither could I see an empty boat carelessly left for my convenience.

Well, the canal would certainly be patrolled. What was the time between each patrol? Carefully hidden in the long grass, I lay and watched and presently they came. Two men and corporal. They passed and returned, passed and returned again. The longest time I could reasonably depend upon was only ten minutes.

The next thing was to find something to help hold me up while swimming across. I could see no signs of any wiring having been done, but I considered that

91

if I had been putting the wire in the canal as a trap, I would have buried the wiring irons to which it was attached. The Germans might have done the same thing. But the wire had to be risked.

I could hear the deliberate stutter of a German Maxim. And then one of our Lewis guns would send its smooth stream of bullets softly whistling overhead in reply.

Coming back a little from the canal I started to look for a log or board or two but the only material I could find that would float was a few wicker shell baskets. These baskets or panniers were made to hold four shells each and to fasten onto a pack-saddle, one on either side. I procured four which were in good enough repair for my purpose. I made a sort of mattress or raft about two feet wide by six in length. With this flimsy aid I resolved to make my attempt.

The night was clear and the moon so high that I considered it best to wait until it had set. While crouching under the hedge waiting for darkness I bethought me of the matter of eats. This was natural enough, since the last of my bread had disappeared during the day while I shivered, wet and cold, among the weeds. All I had left to nibble at were a few horse beans which I had gleaned from a field the night before. Of these I had not more than a dozen, so they did not help much. However, I was not so very hungry. My increasing nervousness acted as a substitute for food. In many ways this was the most dangerous hazard of the whole attempt.

I might drown through sheer inability to get across. Or I might get hooked by the wire and drown that way. I might get tangled and provide target practice for the patrol or I might get safely across only to climb out of the canal into the waiting arms of a patrol on the other side. The next half hour promised to be interesting!

92

Chapter Eight

Slowly the moon lowered, its colour shading gradually from white to yellow and then, just as it disappeared, to a rich orange. Unlacing my boots I secured them to the front end of my raft. I waited still a little longer, until the night was as dark as it would get. The next time the Germans passed, I would go. My excitement rose higher as the moments crawled.

Presently I heard their heavy footfalls as the patrol thumped toward me, their boots scuffing the gravel along the tow-path. They came abreast. They passed on . . . One hundred paces . . . One hundred and fifty.

Now! I rose, cautiously, lifting my awkward contraption which wobbled and creaked alarmingly. Up the bank, over the path and I launched my frail craft. Sitting on the bank I slid gently into the icy water, flopping forward onto the shell-baskets as I did so.

They proved to be quite buoyant, in fact too much so, and I wriggled back off them a little to avoid being upset. In spite of my best efforts I made a certain amount of noise. Being partly out of the water my arms dripped at every stroke, and my legs made a little splash.

I was getting on fine and was just thanking my

stars that the wire scare was only a rumour when I felt something catch my leg. It did not stop me at once, but I knew I was hooked. Swiftly backing water I reached down with one arm and attempted to disengage the barbs. With a little trouble I did so, but as the wire dropped it caught my other leg. Frantically I worked and tore myself free once more.

On again, splashing and swimming desperately in an effort to make up the lost time . . . Only twenty yards to go . . . fifteen . . . Suddenly I heard heavy boots pounding along the tow-path behind me. Hoarse shouts . . . What to do? What to do? I still kept doggedly paddling . . . Again the challenge. They would fire now . . . Dear God!

Ten yards yet . . . And in my eagerness to get to shore I dropped my feet too soon and was promptly snagged again. Crack! A bullet cut the water with a little "plunk" close to my head. I rolled off my support and lowered my body out of sight.

Crack! Crack! The whole party now opened fire, while I tore at my trapped leg. Suddenly the wire gave way. The next time the bullet struck the water near me, I gave a cry, ending it with my mouth near the surface. This probably sounded pretty horrible and as if I were badly hit. I wasn't quite sure that a man hit in the head would act that way, but the chances were my friends on the bank were no better informed. However, the ruse worked, and the firing ceased.

I gave a few more convulsive splashes in the right direction to make the play realistic and then lay still. That is, nearly still, as my hands kept paddling me gently nearer the shelter and safety of the bank. I could hear the Germans talking together on the tow-path, and presently, just as my head bumped softly against the stone coping, two of them struck off back the way they had come leaving one of their number on the bank opposite me.

Carefully unfastening my boots from the raft I gently pushed it as far out as I could and had the satisfaction of seeing what little current there was catch it and move it slowly away downstream.

After about twenty minutes I heard steps and voices coming along on my side. Getting a hail from the man opposite, his two companions who had crossed by the bridge or boat farther down, came abreast, and I could hear them talking within a few feet of my head. I was, however, fairly well hidden, my face being all that was above water and it was sheltered beneath an overhanging tuft of grass.

While they stood so close to me, I hardly dared to breathe for fear of making a ripple that would give me away. I was so cold I could have yelled in agony. Presently they spotted my raft which had drifted twenty or thirty yards downstream. They walked down and stood opposite that for a while, shouting back and forth to one another. Then to my intense relief they all moved away. I waited where I was for another half hour or so to give anyone who was suspicious time to get impatient and clear out. Slowly, then, numbed with the cold, my teeth chattering so that I could hardly keep them still, I gradually pulled myself out of the water and to the top of the bank. All seemed safe.

This side of the canal was swampy, as I soon discovered. I had not proceeded very far through the willows and grass-grown hummocks before I stepped into a black slimy pool that seemed without bottom. As I felt myself going I flung my weight backwards onto the solid ground behind me. Then, twisting around and gripping the grass rushes, I pulled myself to safety again.

I set my feet down with more care. The swamp or muskeg grew worse the further I penetrated its depths. The whole area seemed like a huge lake that had grown over with vegetation. Every step I sank knee-deep, and the surface on all sides rippled in long, shuddery waves at every movement. Time and again I plunged through the thin sod with one foot and was only able to extricate myself with the greatest difficulty.

I wanted to find a solid place where I could dry myself somewhat but I feared that when I found the solid spot, I would also discover that it was already a machine-gun post. At any rate, after a time, I did find a small, fairly solid bit of uninhabited ground around the base of a willow bush. I peeled off my saturated clothes, wrung them out and put them on again. That done, as silently as possible, I swung my arms, kicked my legs and threw my body about in an effort to restore circulation and finish drying my clothes. A fire, welcome beyond words, was quite out of the question.

While doing this I considered whether to keep going west during the remainder of the night and take a chance with the boggy mess surrounding me or lay up until daylight and try to worm my way through the hummocks on my stomach, The fact that I was hungry, cold and wet decided me to keep moving as long as I could. So presently, having warmed myself somewhat by my furious exercise, I stole forward again.

A few yards, then a long pause to look and listen. Every clump of willows was scrutinized long and carefully before being approached. I was now on what in decent country would be the German front line. I could expect a listening post at every bush. My every step might draw the attention of someone lying perfectly still and watching for the least suspicious movement from any direction.

A German machine-gun a couple of hundred yards to my right front was my least hazard. That caused me no worry. Every now and then it would tear off a burst, and I knew where it was. What did worry me were the machine-guns and listening-posts, if any, in my immediate front. By swinging more to the right and nearer to the machine-gun I could hear, I would remove a certain amount of the unknown danger, as there would not likely be another post close to it.

With this idea in mind I worked over to the right

96

and was nearly abreast of the machine-gun when I was stopped by a long winding sheet of water. I almost called it a stream but I could tell by the slime and scum on the surface that it had no current. It was too wide to jump and when tested with a stick I could not touch bottom. I shrank from the notion of wading or swimming it, as the upper part of me was by now fairly warm and dry. To try and walk around it by the right would take me dangerously close to the machine-gun post, and to the left lay unexplored territory.

While I debated this problem I noticed day had begun to break so after going a little way to the left and not seeing any end to the obstacle I decided to lay up for the day.

Back in the swamp again I found a clump of willows, the base of which was fairly solid ground. Here I pulled a quantity of grass for bedding and cover. I completed my preparations for a comfortable day by wringing out my socks and breakfasting on a few strips of willow bark that proved to be nauseatingly bitter. Fortunately I could move around to a certain extent though I did not dare to stand up.

About ten in the morning it began to rain. The wind also got up, searching behind the meagre shelter and making my unhappy situation ten times worse. The alarming quality of my hunger was weakening my morale. I remembered that the bulbous roots of the big green flags that here abounded were edible, but unluckily there were none at hand by my retreat, and I dare not leave its shelter.

With a warm day and a full belly the situation would have been excellent. Another hour or so of travel would see me safe but in the meanwhile a hot meal and a warm bed somewhere would have been worth ten years of my life.

Every now and then cramps would seize the muscles of my feet and legs, and though I removed my shoes and rubbed my tortured limbs as hard as I could, it helped very little. I tried to get some sleep and succeeded in dozing off occasionally for a few minutes in spite of the bitter wind and constant lash of rain upon my unprotected body. Another age-long day passed by.

Slowly the light grew dim, and bushes which all day long had looked innocent enough gradually appeared as black, shadowy masses which might easily shield an approaching patrol from my sight. The wind and rain which seemed as bad as ever offset the increased brilliance of the moon. In fact if there had been no moon at all behind the scudding clouds, the darkness would have been so impenetrable that I doubt if I could have travelled in that swamp at all. As it was I started out again heading toward the strip of open water.

Reaching it, since I was soaked already in any case, with no more ado, I let myself down into the oozy depths and struck out for the other bank.

It was horrible stuff to swim in, thick and clinging, but I managed to keep my legs high and though for a while I thought I would not make it, I gradually worked my way through it and at last grasped the sod on the other bank and pulled myself out.

The sheet or sod of grass roots was thinner here than on the side I had just left, and as I tried to raise myself, it sank down immersing me almost to waist depth again. However by dint of very careful crawling and scrambling I succeeded in gaining more solid ground without breaking through the flimsy layer with more than one foot at a time.

Without relaxing my caution I worked my way forward, until the machine-gun was directly on my right. Here the going improved considerably; the pools were fewer and presently ceased altogether. The ripple and the quake of the muskeg gave way to ordinary marsh grassland, and I proceeded more slowly and carefully than ever as by the sound of the Lewis gun in front and the position of the German Maxim I guessed I was in No-Man's-Land.

The country was still too marshy for trenches so I

judged what line there was would be formed of listening posts. For these the many clumps of willow would be ideal. Of the two brands of listening posts I considered the British as being the most hazardous for me, since I would be approaching from the German lines. To the Germans I would be coming from their rear and would be assumed to be a friend unless my suspicious movements gave me away. The Germans would probably challenge, but I doubted that the British would under the circumstances. I could just imagine some fed-up Tommy lying on his stomach watching me sneaking towards him and saying to himself, "Now when the blighter gets up to that bunch of grass I'll let him have it."

Step by cautious step. Nearer and ever nearer to friends and safety and food. Oh, heaps of it! Cans of delicious bully beef; pockets-full of good solid army biscuit! I tore my mind from the picture. That later, perhaps. In the meantime, caution. Caution.

What was that? A voice to the left rear! I froze instantly, sinking slowly down and glancing over my shoulder to appraise the danger. It was a patrol of four or five Germans and they were headed to pass me within ten yards. Too close for comfort and I started to worm my way over to the right where there was a sort of hedge-row of large willows. I was almost up to the shelter of these when I saw a slight movement ahead. I froze again and sank low. Too late!

"*Wer da?*" Silence, while I thought rapidly on how to keep him from shooting.

"*Wer da?*" more sharply.

"*Un ami!*" I answered in French . . . I would be a farmer from behind his own lines.

"*Hier kommen!*" I rose to my feet and explaining in French that I was lost, calmly walked toward the German who had also stood up keeping me covered with his Luger as he did so.

As I came close to him, and he could see very well that I was no French peasant, I dropped all pretence, once past the danger point, and suggested that he be my prisoner. I pointed out the advantage of being in a nice safe prison for the duration over the obvious demerits of being a mangled corpse in a shell-hole. If he would get me past the German patrols I would attend to the rest of it.

He heard me out while still holding the Luger pointed at my middle with a hand that trembled alarmingly. When I paused, he answered my generous proposition with a surly grunt: Nothing doing! Or words to that effect.

I returned to the attack, telling of the plentiful supplies of good food - I waxed enthusiastic about that - the comfortable, warm, dry beds, the flesh-pots of Paris when the war was over. I watched his face keenly, while he weighed my offer...

Of a sudden I dug my hand down into a pocket and fished out a sodden bundle. "Fifty marks to boot! How about it?"

But he shook his head. He motioned with his revolver for me to sit down. Obediently I sank down on the little bank, suddenly very weary. The urge for freedom that had driven my exhausted body on and ever on to the actual verge of safety, had momentarily evaporated. For a time I sat there glooming dully into my cupped hands, elbows on knees, while the German stood watching me warily.

Ah well, the game was up and I had lost. I had certainly done my best and did not see how I should have acted differently. That I had failed was my bad luck rather than my bad management. This conclusion helped my self-esteem.

My captor was still alone, the party I had been dodging when I ran into him having gone on without seeing or hearing anything. Presently he sat down beside me and offering a drink from his canteen proceeded to get acquainted. I guzzled his hot, sweet coffee gratefully and remarked superfluously that the war was *"nicht gut, huh?"*

He agreed somewhat reservedly, seeming to fear

that if he showed too much distaste of the war I might renew my insidious campaign. I soon learned that he was awaiting the return of a machine-gun patrol of which he was the corporal. From time to time he would gaze off through the grey drizzle impatiently looking for their appearance. I knew well enough what the fiction hero of adventure stories would do in my case. During a momentary lapse of his watch over me I would spring upon him. A short, fierce struggle and I would continue on leaving the German either dead or unconscious, bound securely with his shoe laces. But after considering the matter I finally chucked the idea. For one thing he had let me live at the distinct risk to himself, since it would have been much safer for him to have fired first and enquired afterwards. He was not to know that I was unarmed when I advanced toward him with my hands at my sides, talking soldier French. Another thing, he knew I had money, and German money at that, yet he did not attempt to take it or search me for other valuables. Besides, I was not sure that if I started anything I could successfully finish it. A touch of dysentery topped off with a goodish spell of short rations, long walks and wet clothes, knocks a lot of fighting ability and spirit from a man. One more thing and I thought of it with a faint grin as I looked at his boots - he hadn't any shoe laces and I needed mine. No, I'd lost the game and would abide by the decision.

We sat there in the rain together for another hour or more, then, apparently deciding that his party had returned by some other route he gave the word and we started for the rear. For a time he kept me pretty closely covered but after we had plodded on together for a mile or two he grew to think me a harmless sort of dub and put his gun back in its holster.

He was really very decent. Gave me a cigarette now and then; and when I told him I was hungry he begged some bread for me from another post which we passed.

We skirted the edge of the swamp until we struck a road that crossed it. This road led us to a bridge over the canal about half a mile down from where I had crossed.

We came to a village where he conducted me to his billet. As we had passed through two or three villages on our way, he could have handed me over to the military police, but I suspected he wanted to parade the captive before his own little crowd. When we climbed the ladder into the dark loft, he called for a candle, as he had a *Tommee gefangennen* to bed down for the night. His announcement met nothing but a few derisive snorts.

However, he did finally get a light and I was immediately subjected to an inspection by all present who promptly tumbled up to have a look at the exhibit. When curiosity had been well satisfied, and the corporal had told his tale at least twice, he hunted up a blanket and mattress for me, and the rest of the night I slept like the dead.

The next morning he took me downstairs to his lieutenant who was having breakfast. The officer was a handsome youngster of about my own age who could speak excellent English with only the slightest caress when he pronounced his V's.

After dismissing the corporal and waving me to a seat he asked me what I was doing along their front line, and I answered with a certain amount of truth that I was looking for his machine-gun outposts. I had made up my mind that if possible I would pose as a newly-captured prisoner, then if I were sent to a different concentration camp I might be able to dodge what punishment was due me for having broken out.

When I told him that many people overseas believed that if the Germans won they would dominate the world, he said, "Why, man, can't your people get it into their heads that Germany is fighting for her life? She is hemmed in with your triple Entente and her back is to the wall."

102

"What about the violation of Belgium's neutrality in 1914?" I asked coldly.

He sighed wearily: "Yes, you people always use that as an excuse to get into the war. You ignore the fact that Belgium is strongly French in sentiment, and that a secret treaty exists between those two nations which allows the French, in the event of war with Germany, to cut across Belgium in order to get us in the flank. Because we cut across first, the Allies raise their hands in holy terror. Even the Belgian fortresses of Liege and Namur were designed and built under the direction of French artillery engineers. You hadn't heard about that, eh?"

I shook my head in silence not knowing what to say to this. What was the truth? Did the Germans honestly believe that their side was in the right? It did indeed seem so.

"Oh, well, " he went on, "it's all a terrible mess no matter who or what the outcome will be. By the way," he broke off, "did those fellows upstairs give you any breakfast?"

"No," I grinned, "I suspect they sent me down here out of the way, while they were having their own."

"Quite likely," he agreed. Cutting a generous portion from the loaf of white bread on the table, he smeared it well with butter and passed it to me with the remark, "Their rations are barely enough for themselves."

As I took his offering I confessed ruefully, "I almost persuaded your corporal last night that prisoners' bread was better than the German rations, but he was too good a soldier for me."

The officer stared for a moment. "You were captured by him and then tried to persuade him to be your prisoner," a smile broadening his face.

"Uh-huh. I even offered him a bunch of money besides but it was no go. He didn't seem to like the idea."

The German laughed in keen enjoyment at this and knocked on the floor for his orderly, "Kaporal

Scholtz," he commanded. In a few moments my captor appeared and saluted from the doorway. The officer repeated what I had just told him at which the corporal nodded and blushed. He added a few words of his own which seemed to suit the other immensely.

Then after giving instructions where to take his prisoner the officer turned to me: "You are a brafe man," he remarked. "I like you, goodbye and good luck for the future." And then believe it or not, he shook my hand!

Well, I thought, as the corporal and I struck out for Denain, they may be Huns and blonde beasts and woman murderers and what not, I certainly never heard of one of our officers shaking hands with a German private.

For a time I felt a bit guilty about fooling such a decent sort of chap with my answer to his question of what I was doing on the line, but after thinking the matter over, I decided that I was only fooling myself. For one thing, I was unarmed when captured. Also my coloured shoulder badges from one side were missing - they had been removed at the Intelligence Bureau at Lewarde. Moreover he had not made the slightest attempt for information, which, if he had believed me to be newly captured, he would almost certainly have done.

No, I think he was smart enough to know my game and yet was a good enough sport not to ask awkward questions. If I could work the bluff with the prison authorities and get away with it, it was all right with him. May his shadow grow wider!

Our first stop - barring a few at wayside canteens - was at the Intelligence Bureau at Denain. Here a German sergeant took my name, number and regiment. I gave correct answers believing that I was doing the double on them. He then asked me with what Brigade, division, army corps we were attached and at this I balked, not knowing how much it would help them to know. At my attitude both of the others laughed scornfully.

104

"Don't be foolish," said the sergeant, "we know all we wanted to know as soon as you had been reported. I asked you merely to keep up to date on your nice little colour scheme. "Look," he went on, "I'll show you." Taking down a large book about the size of a banker's ledger, he laid it on the table. Riffling over a few pages he came to the one he sought. "Iss not that very pretty?" He pointed to row after row of our shoulder colours. He picked out the one belonging to my own regiment. "Zare you are! A green half moon above a French grey rectangle and you need not tell me a sing. Your regiment is the second in seniority in the seventh brigade, third division. See I tell YOU!" The colours were exact to a shade. Cap badges, some modest like that of our regiment, others, a bit loud. Brass shoulder badges commonly worn by the various units were all reproduced exactly as to shape and size.

He seemed very proud of the effect his disclosures were making on me and turned over some more pages. New Zealand, Australia, Scottish, Indian, and page after page of Imperial regimental colours were all reproduced with the most exacting fidelity.

"Wheneffer we want to know what troops you have in the line we take one little look through a field-glass and if we see only one shoulder colour, we know all. Much easier and better than a raid for information, *nicht wahr*?" After assuring him that as far as I knew his picture book was quite up to date, we left for Lewarde. I inwardly boiled. It was true enough. All along I had had a suspicion that whichever brass-tabbed nincompoop first thought out that shoulder colour scheme certainly put in a good day's work for old Fritz.

What earthly good to us were those colours anyway? Surely it wasn't necessary for one of our generals to go out on the raid and examine the shoulders of the troops marching by in order to find out who they were. Surely the junior officers and the buck privates could do their various jobs without knowing the regiment, brigade and so on of a man walking across a field one hundred yards away! It had me beat.

They might have a made it easier for the military police to pick up a deserter, but aside from that meagre benefit to the cause, I could think of no good reason for the things being worn.

At the Intelligence Office in Lewarde the corporal handed me over to the officer in charge and departed. To my surprise this man promptly recognized me as having been there before and demanded an explanation. Realizing that the game was up, and it was now no further use trying to pass as newly captured, I told him straight that I had escaped, got as far as the line, been nabbed by the machine-gun chap who had delivered me and here I was again.

He shook his head in wonder at one who would deliberately leave the shelter of a prison and take a chance on the front line once more. "Whatever did you want to escape for? Is it not better to be a prisoner than in the trenches?"

He seemed earnestly desirous of learning why I escaped so I told him of the short rations, the filth and the sickness. I also told him of my deep longing to return home and to be done with war and soldiers; that as an escaped prisoner I would not again be required to take my place in the front line.

When I was finished he kept silence for a space then said quietly: "I don't blame you for escaping. I am sure I would do the same were I in your place. But," he added as he opened the guardroom door, "I hope you will not try to get away from here."

"I'll give you my parole on that if you like," I offered. "The moon is far too bright just now for another attempt."

He laughed at that and called the guard to bring me something to eat. In a little while that worthy returned with a huge tinful of rich soup and meat besides a generous issue of black bread. The bread I cached away for the lean days ahead but the soup I cleaned up to the last spoonful much to the wonder and admiration of the guard. The officer also sent me in a late copy of the *London Times*.

In the evening I was given a good bed of clean hay and three or four blankets, and I slept for a solid fourteen hours.

Chapter Nine

The next morning after a generous breakfast of bread and honey I stood at the door of the bull-pen, and when Madame, my old acquaintance, appeared, I gave her a cheerful hail and asked if I could borrow her razor again.

The good soul was astounded to see me back and wanted to know all about it, but the guard was rather officious just then and kept rudely interrupting. However, I soon got around that. I wrote her a letter behind the half-raised page of the "Times" and posted it to her in a chink under the window ledge, catching her eye and pointing out the note when the guard was looking the other way. She wrote me a reply by return post and also sent me a clean pair of socks and a towel and soap, so that I was able to get cleaned up once more.

After lunch that day a couple of small and rather aged Germans escorted me back to Denain where I was lodged in a large prison barracks. On my way down my guards had their wind up over me to a most gratifying degree. They seemed afraid that I would start something, daylight and all, and kept a rifle trained in my direction most of the time. We travelled by steam tram, and on the way I tried to buy some cigars from a couple of Germans who were going on leave. We were just completing a deal, when an officer butted in and asked what it was I wanted. I told him I was just buying some cigars. "Huh," he snorted . "Zanks to your blockade we haff no tobacco in Chermany any more whateffer!" And he glared at me, until I felt quite ashamed.

At the camp in Denain I was locked in an upper room all to myself, and although I had an excellent spring bed and mattresses, they gave me no supper or breakfast. I kicked up the deuce of a row about that, of course, demanding to see the corporal of the guard, the sergeant of the camp and the Kommandant of the whole town. To all of the fuss raised in the approved old soldier manner I received the usual hard-boiled army answer: "No rations come up for you yet."

I knew all about that to be sure but I also knew that if they wanted to stretch a point, they could always do so. Not that I was suffering in the least. On my various travels during the previous two days I had collected a nice little supply of bread and salt horse which the French civilians had given me. In fact several times during the morning when my incorruptible friend the corporal was taking me to Lewarde, we went into an estaminet for a drink, and he let the civvies fairly load me down with bread. However, I raised old Harry on general principles and at noon got a little action in the way of a big mess-tin of boiled vegetables.

Shortly afterwards, I was taken to the train along with about thirty newly captured C. M. Rs to be shipped to the Fresnes camp. They made no special arrangements for me in the way of extra guards, and when we arrived we were all turned loose inside the lager just like any other bunch of ordinary prisoners. They either forgot about the black sheep or the guards from Denain had no record of one. A policy of meekness for a few days seemed to be a good idea.

However, I lost no time in hiking for the *Kammer*

and asking for a blanket or overcoat, along with the others. Cohen, the interpreter, was there handing them out under the supervision of a guard and the camp sergeant.

It was growing dark, but Cohen spotted me all right. He said nothing but grinned, as I took the overcoat he offered me. A little later he slipped me a handful of Red Cross cakes.

After I had located a vacant mattress I hit off to find a few old acquaintances and about the first one I ran across was the corporal who had followed me through the breach in the partition. They had thought I was safe across by this time, since I had been gone so long. I asked after the other two, and he told me that all three of them had been caught the following morning. They had reached the bank of the same canal that I had struck but all three had been picked up shortly after daylight by military policemen. It appeared that not one of them had thought of laying up for the day and they were pinched right out in the open.

We mentioned the Kid. They had reported him shot when they were brought back.

Next morning I fully expected to receive an invitation to visit Hindenburg, the Kommandant. To be perfectly honest about it I had been rather dreading this encounter. Besides his unpleasant Teutonic jib and voice that would make a sick calf click its heels he had a reputation for hot and heavy punishment to defaulters. The corporal told me that he and the other two had caught merry blazes after they got back. They were paraded before him and after nearly roaring them to death he had put them to carrying a heavy railroad iron up and down the yard at the double. They had a full hour of this twice a day for several days and were sentenced to two weeks' solitary confinement as soon as the "pens" were completed.

He showed me a place by the cookhouse where several brick dog kennels had been built. They were just high and long enough so that a man could neither sit nor stand nor lie in comfort inside them. In size they would be about three feet high by three feet wide by five feet long, and with a heavy plank door at the end. After looking them over I came to the conclusion that anyone who had two weeks in one of those would be willing to be a good little boy afterwards. I didn't imagine the inmates would be supplied with a mattress or blanket, and the brick floor would strike hard and cold to our skinny frames.

When several days had gone by without the expected invitation to visit his nibs, I came to the conclusion that the Intelligence Officer at Lewarde had passed me on to the Denain people without any comments as to my previous record, and they had taken it for granted that I was newly captured. Cohen had also kept quiet, and the German camp-sergeant had not recognized me. Any irregularities in the nominal roll could be corrected by Cohen who was the unofficial orderly corporal.

I had asked the officer at Lewarde what punishment I could expect. He had looked grave and said he understood it was very severe. I neither asked for, nor did he make any promise to help me, but it is certain that by some lucky break I missed punishment of any sort for trying to escape.

The first week or two after getting back I had a pretty thin time of it. I felt lonesome and blue. How I hated those dirty soldiers! The sound of them, the sight of them, the stench of them sickened my very soul, and for the most part I kept to my mattress and slept away as many of the weary hours as I could.

Then one day shortly after dinner, the little cockney corporal who previously had worked in the cookhouse came and sitting down beside me, asked me if I could do with a bit of "buckshee vedge." I promptly passed him my empty mess-tin with the ungracious remark, "Your move, old-timer."

He dumped half the contents of his tin into mine and these I gulped without further delay. It appeared he had fallen out with Wilhelm, the German head

112

cook, but he still had a friend in the cookhouse who occasionally passed him out a soup bone or an extra ladle of boiled vegetables.

After we had scraped the last morsel of food from our tins, he leaned back and fished from an inside pocket a small volume which I immediately recognized as a Testament. I started, wondering for a moment if he were going to hold a prayer meeting, but from another hiding place he hauled a small cotton sack which proved to contain the dried leaves from which our "tea" had been made. In his palm he kneaded and crushed a pinch of the leaves which, after he had detached a half page from the Testament, he proceeded to roll into a cigarette.

"Ere y'are," he remarked, giving it to me. "Service, we calls it. All modern conveniences and luxuries in our hotel. Awftah dinnaw the gentlemen repaired to the saloon wheaw they enjoyed cigaws and cocktails. On'y just now we're aht o' cocktails, sir."

He was a smart little fellow with hair so yellow it was almost white. He had been a sailor before the mast aboard a schooner. He had been cook below deck. He had wrestled merchandise on the wharves at Wapping and had, among a few other exciting vocations, been at one time apprenticed to a gang of burglars! The latter he had "chucked" because, he was at pains to explain, "it was a fool's game." He had also been married but had chucked that also and for the same reason.

On every other topic his viewpoint was always merry, and what with his cheeriness and the frequent scraps of food that he brought in and shared with me, I soon thawed out and would sit up and wag my tail in welcome when he appeared.

He was very good to me for no particular reason that I could see and he finally dug me out of my blue devils and got us both a job on a fatigue party going up into the village every day. He was a wonder at "scrounging" as he called it. The American synonym for the verb "to scrounge" is to "rustle." It may mean

113

to beg, to find, to buy at a bargain, to have given to one and even to steal but the sense in the two words is the same which is "to get."

I soon proved to him that when I set my mind to it I was rather a good hand at that game myself, though when my low cunning failed to get results, I was prone to draw upon my small hoard of cash, while the Corp would nearly always score solely by the charm of his manner.

He had had very little schooling in his youth - a typical London gutter-snipe. What learning he had received in his childhood he put to good account later, reading and studying anything and everything he could get. He was much better versed in both ancient and modern writers than I was by a long shot.

On our way to and from work a field-grey column would swing past singing. Often we got a cheerful hail from the ranks: "Hi, Tommee, come on back to the line with us." Or: "Long way to Tipperary, Tommee, *nicht wahr*?" Few of the Germans were between the ages of twenty and thirty-five. The majority were either well over that age or around seventeen or eighteen. Many looked to be over fifty.

Their horse transports, like those of the French, were strictly utilitarian and looked the worse for wear. Every horse pulled all it could handle, and man-power was cut to a minimum.

Motor transports and ambulances were the same, reasonably clean and ship-shape but without evidence of the under-carriage being washed and polished before starting out on the day's work, as was the custom in our transports.

After the Corp had taken up with me he moved his mattress over alongside mine, and at night after we had eaten our rations and "scroungings" and drunk our warm beech-leaf tea we'd lie side by side in the darkness and talk.

Soldiers as a class have two major topics of conversation: liquor and women. We in the prison camp were marked departures from this rule. Our desires

114

were more fundamental. We thought food; we dreamed food; we talked food. Not cakes or pastries or fried oysters, but huge slabs of fat pork, solid loaves of army bread, gobs of butter and chunks of cheese. Since conversation pertaining to food inevitably led to England for the Corp and overseas for me, it was only to be expected that before we had been talking very long, our discussions would swing around to ways and means of escape.

To him I unfurled a theory or two which I had developed along the line of prison-breaking. He nodded agreement when I pointed out the importance of arranging the actual moment of getting unstuck so that one would not get shot in doing it.

"Jolly sound idea," he said, carefully tearing out John 2, chapter 4 and rolling a cigarette. "Got a match? Thanks." He puffed in silence a while and then, "What about stowing away aboard one of those junk barges going up to Antwerp? No chance of a bullet in a go of that sort is there?"

I considered. "Not that I can see at the moment. But how about grub? It'd be a pretty lengthy trip. And how would you get the guards to think we had hidden anywhere but in the barge, if we turned up missing at the end of the day?"

The Corp went on planning aloud: "We could pinch a boat, get to Holland or p'raps out to sea and get picked up by a mine-sweeper..."

"Or a mine or maybe a U-boat," I suggested helpfully.

"Crickey," whispered the little cockney, not paying me the least attention, "I wouldn't arf like to feel that old North Sea under foot again!"

I snorted, "Snap out of it, Barnacle Bill. That idea's sour - too many difficulties."

Yet even after we had agreed the scheme was impracticable, our conversation often veered around to it again. We couldn't seem to leave it alone. A good simple method that appealed to us both was to break ranks some evening when we had been delayed until near dark before quitting work. The only thing that deterred me was the fact that our guards were usually pretty decent - stretching discipline as far as possible when civilians offered us food. To break ranks successfully would mean that the guard at the rear of the column would likely get into heavy trouble with the Kommandant and perhaps be returned to the trenches. We did not anticipate that the escort at the head of the party would be held to blame, as he could hardly be expected to both lead and keep an eye on what was going on behind him.

However, this little problem in prison ethics solved itself one day. The Corp and I were on a barge-loading party and our rear-guard for that day, a newcomer to the camp, was rather a stickler for discipline. He didn't believe in letting us smoke tea-leaf cigarettes on the march, nor would he even consider my suggestion that he steal a loaf of bread from the Kommandant and sell it to us. He kept trying to make us walk in step and salute the officers and such-like frightfulness. One got the impression that he was trying to win a stripe, and as a consequence nobody loved him.

This chap on the particular day I'm telling of spotted a young Imperial accepting a couple of raw potatoes from a woman who lived in the row of houses that fronted on the canal. Cursing horribly, he ran up and struck the English lad over the head with his rifle. Then with the butt he hit the woman in the chest causing her to stumble and fall to the ground.

She screamed, and though neither she nor the young Britisher were greatly hurt, the German was pretty well mobbed by a number of other women who ran out of their houses when they heard the uproar. Our other guard came running to help chase off the other women who were shrieking to high heaven for immediate vengeance.

At the time the ruckus started I had been conning over in my mind ways and means of a get-away. Reluctance to make serious trouble for our guards, difficulty of getting away without being shot at and the problem of getting out of the enemy-occupied area of Belgium made a puzzle that wouldn't fit together.

At the woman's screams the Corporal had growled to me: "Come on!" and started over to join the riot, but for once I had a spasm of discretion. Also the glimmering of an idea.

"Here, wait!" And I grabbed him by the shoulder. While the Germans were quieting the trouble, we went into a huddle. At the sight of the frenzied women and the brutal guard, matters had suddenly clicked into shape. The Corp grinned and nodded agreement.

The German in charge then ordered everyone to get to work and have done with chattering and fooling about. The barges we were loading were nearly full, and if necessary they would keep us working until the job was done, even though it was after dark when we finished. But just to make sure we did not finish too early the Corp and I moved quietly among our fellow-toilers spreading the insidious gospel of *"Nix Brodt, nix Arbeit!"* This was Tommy-German for "No extra bread, no hard work!"

Since my first attempt at escape I had grown to have some appreciation for the hate which the majority of the civilians entertained for the Germans. I learned that there was not the slightest risk of one of them betraying an escaping prisoner who appealed to them for aid. If they could not or dared not aid him they certainly would not assist in his recapture. Although the maximum penalty for helping an escaped prisoner was death, that did not deter many civilians from lending all possible aid to Allied soldiers trying to get out of the country. While the extreme penalty was held over their heads, it was pretty well understood that only in the case of wholesale deliberate flouting of this rule - as in the matter of Nurse Cavel - would it be inflicted. But it was also well understood that anyone caught harbouring an escaping prisoner would certainly be in for a bunch of trouble. And only those who were either strongly patriotic or had some extra special grudge against the Germans could be expected to lend such aid as we had in mind to ask. This woman who had been assaulted would, I figured, be a fairly ripe subject.

Watching my chance I wrote her a little note in which I said that we wanted to send the German who had struck her to the trenches, and if she would like to help us, to be at the rear of her house at about half past nine that night.

Back on the job I kept a sharp lookout for her, but she did not re-appear, and finally I worded it. "To the woman the German struck." Catching the eye of one of her neighbours I slipped the note under a loose brick where we got our drinking water. Next time I went for a drink the note was gone. Two women were standing in a doorway looking rather frightened, and one of them was the Madame I wanted. The one who had seen me hide the note pointed me out to the other, and I asked my question with eyebrows. She nodded nervously, and they both went inside.

We industriously set to work to loaf on the job so that it was really quite dark when we finished. After we had been lined up, numbered off and found correct we marched off in double file, our two guards taking the same stations at the head and rear of the column as they had occupied in the morning. So far so good.

The tendency of soldiers when marching in file at night is to follow the man in front and watch your footing. I figured that our son of Bismarck at the rear, after possibly keeping a fair watch over us for the first quarter mile or so would lapse back into his accustomed practice, and the Corp and I could dodge off quietly and leave him to face the music.

Being late, the guard in front was hitting a good clip, anxious for his sausage and saurkraut probably, and some of the men behind us were saying "Pass the word up, 'Step short in front.'" This message, however, never got nearer the head of the column than the Corp and me. With us it seemed to die off and disappear, the result being that by the time we came to a stretch of rough ground where our path made a shortcut across some fields the line was strung out very thin and ragged indeed.

The night was moonless but starlit, and glancing back I had no difficulty in glimpsing our rearguard with slung rifle mooching along some seventy yards behind us. We had decided to leave about half way across this short cut. Zero hour again!

I was just screwing up my courage to give the Corp a nudge when I noticed three or four Germans approaching along another path that would intercept our party. As we were strung out so badly, they would very likely cut right through us rather than wait until we had gone past. For a moment I thought they were going to spoil our game but suddenly recollected a trick from the book of experience.

Over my shoulder I whispered to the Corp to turn his cap around and unfasten his brass buttons, lapping them underneath. The Germans, as I guessed they would, cut right through our column just ahead of me. As we came up to their path I gently murmured to the Corporal, "Left turn, old soldier," leading the way.

The man behind him exclaimed, "Hi, there, you're going the wrong way."

"Shut your gawp," hissed the Corporal, "and keep the line closed up." Still maintaining our ordinary pace we turned and followed a few yards in the rear of the Germans, until we were sure we had not been missed, when we angled off to the left soon losing sight of both parties who continued their ways without halting.

"Pretty neat, I calls it," remarked the Corporal as we struck back for Conde.

"And not a shot fired," I added complacently. "If either the guards or the Heinies in front had noticed us, we had only to look naturally stupid, and the mistake would have been rectified with nothing worse happening to us than a hearty cursing."

In a little while we arrived at the rear of the row of houses that fronted onto the canal. Hiding in the shadow of a low hedge that bordered a garden we waited for our lady to make her appearance.

Ten minutes, half an hour passed and no sign of Madame though every few minutes we could hear a woman a few doors down come out and call her dog.

"Fido seems to be among the missing tonight," I whispered.

"What's his name, anyway? It sounded like Sultan," commented the Corp.

"It does a bit," I agreed. "Let's wriggle up a little nearer and see what it sounds like then."

Presently out she came again though there was no light in the house behind her, a rather singular circumstance I thought. When she called again we could hear her quite distinctly:

"*Ici, Soldat. Ici*! Good old fellow! Come here then!"

"Say, I'll bet you she's calling us," suddenly hissed the Corp.

"Well, she may at that," I agreed "But why so coy about it? Wherefore all the camouflage?"

"Maybe she's scared."

Although we both felt pretty certain she was calling us we felt wary of showing ourselves.

"Here, *Soldat! Soldat*! Come here, old fellow," called the voice again.

"Hey, pal," whispered the Corp. "You're supposed to know all about animals. Can't you make a noise like a four-legged soldier that's a bit shy?"

"Well, I can give a fairly good cat-call if necessary and for that matter she may be calling her pet tom-cat for all we know."

"Go on then," urged my companion. "Let's hear it."

"MIEAOW! MIEAOW!" I wailed in what I hoped sounded like the seductive mating call of a wandering milk-hound.

"Poor Pussy," soothed the Corp, stroking me gen-

120

tly down the back. "Poor old Thomas. Did ums den!"

"*Ici, Soldat, ici!*"

"Mieaow! Mieaow!"

"Dear old Puss . . ." I kicked him savagely in the shin, and while he was rubbing the spot ruefully, we distinctly heard the woman chuckling to herself in the doorway.

"Come on, you idiot. It's us she's calling all right," said I, rising.

As we appeared, the woman stepped back. "*Entrez, soldats,*" she invited with a nervous little laugh and locked the door behind us. "Follow me. We go below where it is safer." She lit a candle and led the way down into the cellar where she bade us make ourselves at home while she fetched something for us to eat. She took it for granted that we were hungry.

While she was gone we made certain that no light could escape through any unguarded chink. Reappearing in a few minutes with a tray of food, the woman arranged it on a couple of boxes.

"*Voilà, messieurs,*" she invited, making the gesture which to all the world means, "Dig in."

When we had satisfied our hunger, we told Madame her German would certainly be up on the carpet in the morning for having let us get away, and that very likely he would be sent back to the trenches as punishment for his negligence. As we expected, the prospect of this pleased her mightily. In fact she fairly gloated over the idea that he would probably be killed in the immediate future. She showed us the not particularly lurid bruise on her chest where the rifle butt had struck her, and we ts'cked our tongues against our teeth in sympathy.

She was oldish - thirty or more, I'd say, with a face and full-bosomed figure that with only a reasonable amount of attention and adornment might have been beautiful.

The fate of the "*sale Boche*" as Madame called him being settled to the satisfaction of all present, I proceeded to the business of dragging in a certain little plan which the Corp and I had been discussing. We told her we wanted to get to the coast, steal a boat and get across to England. We thought Antwerp would be the best port to head for, and had she any suggestions as to the best way to get there.

She did not see why we wanted to go to Antwerp or anywhere. She would gladly let us stay hidden with her for the duration but the Corp put in with the announcement that I was but newly married on my last leave, and that recently my wife had given birth to twins, and I was mad to get over to them! This brought immediate results, and the kind soul bent her mind to the problem of thinking out the best way to get to the coast.

After a few moments she was struck by a brilliant notion: *"Mais oui,"* she cried enthusiastically, "My sister's husband goes to Antwerp in the morning on the barges and perhaps . . . But we shall see." saying which, she bustled off.

"Pretty crummy, I calls it," I growled, "working up the poor woman's sympathies over my imaginary family to gain your own sordid ends. You ought to be jolly well ashamed of yourself." And I frowned reprovingly at him.

"Huh!" snorted the Corp with a grin. "You can say a lot, you unscrupulous blighter."

Very soon our hostess returned followed by her acquaintance of the morning and a tough looking customer in civvies. In rapid-fire French, much too fast for me to do more than get the drift, she outlined her scheme to the man she addressed as Victor. He didn't like the idea in the least, which failed to surprise me very much, but Madame and her sister solved difficulties a good deal faster than he could think of them. Finally he gave up the struggle and set his own wits to work to aid us.

When all seemed to be agreed, Madame turned to us and said, "Victor says there are two Germans in charge of the barges, also another Frenchman beside himself will go, too. Both Germans live on the front boat and the Frenchmen on the last. He says you find a place to hide on the one in front of his."

"How many barges will there be in the tow?" I asked the Corp.

"Four." Victor evidently understood our brand of French. We then addressed our remarks to him and promptly began asking about bread supplies, a system of communication and other information, very much to the pleasure of our hostess who felt immensely gratified that we were falling in so readily with her scheme.

Victor said we would have to keep covered up all day and all night, too, as the Germans mounted a guard over the barges each night, and as we would be on the move all day we might be seen from the shore if we stirred about.

When they stopped overnight at some locks or in a large town, the two Germans usually depended on the local guards to keep an eye on the barges and would turn in for the night. These occasions would be the only chances Victor would have of getting us bread. If we badly wanted help for anything, I had to do the pussy-cat act again, and he would get in touch with us at the first opportunity.

It went without saying that in case of discovery we were hiding quite on our own account and had nothing whatever to do with the boatmen on board.

To get into the barge was the next problem, since Victor said one of the Germans was out on sentry-go at that moment. After some discussion it was agreed that Victor would engage the guard in conversation and try and get him down below-deck for a moment to give us time to slip across and get hidden. We thought just before dawn would be the best time for that, as it was customary to get an early start, and his appearance at that hour would not be unusual.

Just before dawn Victor appeared with a loaf of German bread which we cut up and hid in our pockets. Madame gave us a cup of hot coffee and some French bread and butter for breakfast, though we were not at all hungry - nervousness and excitement, I suppose. She also filled a German water canteen with coffee for us to take along.

Victor was going to take a sack of fresh vegetables aboard for the German escorts. He would try and get the one on guard to go below with him to show where it should be placed. If he could manage that, it would give us the opportunity to sneak aboard.

We bade goodbye to Madame and her sister. I left them my notes to mail out after the war in case I was shot in the meantime. They seemed loth to have us go, shed a tear or two and would not be put off with a mere hand-clasp. We promised to write and visit them again "aprez la guerre" as soldiers do - took down their names and addresses, kissed them again, a good one each for gratitude and left them.

Chapter Ten

The women quietly closed the door after us, and we crept softly a few yards behind Victor, who with his sack of vegetables on his shoulder clip-clopped down the echoing road making row enough to be heard half a mile away. When we heard the sentry challenge him, we crouched silently beside the low wall by the canal edge. Victor growled out his answer and walked on up to the German.

"Put them down beside the gang-plank," we heard the guard say. The Corp and I looked at each other in dismay.

"My old woman says I've got to bring the sack back toute de suite."

"*Egal*, empty them under the foot of the stairs then." Another pause. Then against the skyline we saw the dim figure of Victor walk over the gang-plank and disappear into the barge.

"What about it, Corp?" I whispered. "Think we can get aboard anyway?"

"Wait a mo', that Frenchman's no fool. He may be able to get that fellow below yet. Ah, listen to that!"

From the barge in which Victor had disappeared came a crash of tinware and dishes followed by lurid curses in muffled French from below and a volley of Deutsch from above. With bitter frankness the German gave to the heavens his opinion of all Frenchmen, especially this one, as he abandoned his post and clattered over the plank to vanish below.

Without a word we two arose and, running swiftly to the barge indicated by Victor, scrambled aboard, while from the craft ahead came muffled sounds of more profanity.

Our conveyance seemed to be plugged tight with junk of all descriptions but up in front we managed to wriggle under the roof or deck. We had no time to straighten the stuff out to allow ourselves a little comfort, as the noise we made would give us away at once. We were content to lay up, well out of sight, and let well enough alone. And mightily uncomfortable we were, too, as odd bits of ironware stuck into us at all angles.

As day broke a faint light trickled through. Sounds, footsteps and voices grew more frequent and finally, after a sort of crescendo of all these, silence fell, and we became aware of a gentle lap-lap of water just in front and below us. We were on our way.

"Yo-ho and a bottle of rum!" quoth the Corp. "A life on the rolling wave . . ."

". . . In a hole about six feet deep." I added. "Westward Ho and take me back to dear old Blighty!" In spite of our discomforts we were feeling pretty good over the success of our plans.

We delayed straightening out our hiding place and making ourselves decently comfortable until, by the sounds outside, we knew we were passing through the next town. It was only with the greatest difficulty that we managed to work our way right down to the floor and could then stretch out our legs to some extent and ease our bruised ribs where the bits of iron had been sticking into them. It took us nearly all day to do it, as we could work only when we knew by the noise outside that we were passing through some town.

126

Slowly the dim light faded, and the barges halted at what seemed like a small village. Gradually the sounds and voices departed leaving only the occasional step of someone strolling up and down whom we took to be one of the Germans on guard. The long night passed wearily, and we slept very little, as it was cold down there below the waterline. We had no blankets, of course, and the hard damp boards under us and the occasional pieces of angle iron which we could not bend or push out of our way seemed to fairly gnaw their way to our thinly covered bones.

Dawn appeared at last, and another day crawled by, the gentle voice of the water lulling us to slumber as often as the ache in our bones awakened us. Our loaf was by this time exhausted, and I decided to wriggle out and signal to Victor as soon as it grew dark enough.

While there was still enough noise around to disguise any movement I made, I worked my way to the open air and peeped cautiously over the edge to see where we were. The town was large. Likely our guards would seize the chance of getting a full night's sleep while they left their job to the bridge guard. Victor would know that our bread would be finished by this time and would have some scheme to provide us with a little food, so I lay in the shadow of some over-hanging machinery and watched the waterfront nightlife, laughing or cursing or flirting up and down.

Presently I noticed a man's figure walking slowly towards me keeping close to the canal's edge. As he drew nearer I fancied I could hear the faint call of a cat. I answered, though keeping well down out of sight in case of mistaken identity. As the man came abreast I heard the cat again, this time quite distinctly. I answered and showed myself above the gunwale. IT WAS A GERMAN AND HE WAS LOOKING RIGHT AT ME!

My heart gave a jump that nearly choked me. He

127

paused and I saw a real cat just the other side of him. We had not been betrayed and there was still a chance! I had brought along my little canteen for some water and this I now dipped into the canal. As the water gurgled into it, I looked up at the German and remarked *"Bo' soir M'sieur."*

"Soir," he returned shortly and moved on, the cat mewing gently and trying to rub itself against his leg. As he strolled slowly out of sight, the sweat broke out of me in a flood. Had I fooled him or not? Should we stay hidden or should we run for it before he had time to get help and return? It was possible that my dirty uniform had not shown up khaki in the dim light. My face must have been pretty grimy and what buttons were visible above the gunwale were very dull. There was still a chance, but I would have to talk to the Corporal at once.

A glance around and I called to my friend who came part way out. In a few hurried sentences I told him what had happened and asked his opinion. After a few moments he said, "I leave it to you. You saw the whole play. Whatever happens I'm with you. If we're nabbed, it's no fault of yours."

Quickly deciding, I told him then to come out and lay beside me. If we saw anyone suspicious coming back from the direction in which the German had disappeared, we would clear out in a hurry. This he did, and we waited anxiously while the minutes slowly passed.

We had not lain there longer than five minutes when we saw another man walking slowly by the barges. We both scanned this fellow pretty keenly and were reasonably sure he was our friend Victor before I gave a soft and seductive cat-call. He it was and with a loaf for us too. He would have passed on, but I told him what had just occurred and asked if he would follow up the way the German had gone and let us know if he saw two or three of them coming back.

His eyes widened with fear in the starlight when

we told him, and he hurried off after the German. In a few minutes we saw him returning as fast as he could travel without drawing attention to himself by actually running. We guessed what was up and had jumped ashore by the time he came up to us.

"Quick!" he gasped, "The guards at the bridge! They've sent three others around behind these houses to cut you off from the other way."

A word of thanks and farewell and we ran down the road as hard as we could go. If we could get past the turning where the heading-off party would enter the road, we would be comparatively safe. Just before we got to it we slackened our pace as we did not wish to run past the turning as the Germans came in sight of the corner. Too late, a rising clatter of heavy boots running over the stone flags warned us we were cut-off. A moment later they appeared in full view just ahead of us. "The game's up." I groaned. "May as well surrender."

On our left was the canal; in front were the Germans, and there were Germans behind us. Our only way of escape was through the row of houses that, like most houses in this part of Europe, opened right on to the street.

While I was stupidly staring at the three oncoming figures, the Corp opened a door beside him and grabbing me by the shoulder remarked, "Come on in. It looks as if it's goin' to rain."

We dodged inside, the Germans not ten yards away. They had seen us, of course, but for a moment did not agree as to which door we had entered. Instead of staying and arguing as we would have wished, they simply opened both doors under dispute and let out a roar calculated to scare us into sight again.

No answer from us, of course, though some voices in a room opening off the hall in which we found ourselves, answered them. The German at the door demanded a light and quick about it. Englishers had just been seen to enter.

We had been quietly feeling our way down the hall

and came to a door at the end, but I could not find the handle. While we both frantically fumbled for it, the German at the front entrance had found a match of his own but as he struck it the head flew off and gave us another second or two.

Feverishly I passed my hand up and down the door coming finally to rest at the place where the knob had been. There was only a small hole there now. The German was striking another match, when the door at the side opened, and another appeared holding a lighted candle. They both saw us and came on with a shout. Luckily neither seemed to be armed.

The light showed me that the door before us was secured by a simple latch situated a foot or two higher than I had been feeling for the handle. As I wrenched it open, the Corp struck the candle from the hands of the nearest German, and we both dashed through and slammed the door after us. We were now in a sort of kitchen as we could judge by the dim light that showed through a window.

"Find the way out, quick!" I cried, "and I'll hold the door." As good luck would have it I had the handle of the latch on my side. All they had with which to pull the door open was a little trigger thing that lifts the latch. The hand-grasp was gone from their side of the door.

In a moment the Corp and I had found the door into the backyard and opened it. I saw what looked to be a pile of tools standing by the wall outside.

"Come on!" he called.

"Wait." I cried, "Pass me a hoe or something with a long handle from there beside the step!" Without any waste of time asking questions he grabbed a tool and ran back to me with it. "Run it through the handle past my fingers, quick!"

In a moment he had done it, securing the door for the time being. We then made a dive for the open air. Outside we found ourselves in a walled-in yard. At the lower end, next the wall, stood a small coop for rabbits or chickens, and without a word we made for it, scrambling up and over the wall like a couple of cats chased by a bull-dog. Just as we disappeared we heard the door give way, and the two Germans came pounding out, shouting to their companions in the next yard.

We dropped to the ground beyond the wall and found ourselves in another backyard. The house immediately in front of us showed a dim light through a window on the ground floor. "Shall we chance it?" I asked, nodding toward the light.

"May as well. If we try a house without a light we'll lose precious moments over a locked door." Saying which he turned the handle, and we stepped inside closing the door behind us just as a girl of about twenty, clad only in her night attire and carrying a lighted candle, entered the kitchen from a door at the side. This was probably the light we had seen through the window and I promptly leaned over and blew it out, as she realized who and what we were.

"*Messieurs!*" she gasped. "*Messieurs!*"

"*Mademoiselle,*" I said in a low voice, "Your pardon but some Germans are after us. Show us the way to the street and then get back into bed." She still stood there, her white nightie making her perfectly visible to us.

"*Vite!*" I hissed at her, "*les Boches sont ici!*"

Their voices I could hear in the yard. They were debating as to whether we had gone into this house or had followed down the row before attempting to escape from the walled-in block of buildings.

My voice, together with those outside brought her to her senses. Quickly running to the door through which we had entered she quietly dropped the latch which locked it. She was probably on her way to do that very thing when we burst in upon her. She then beckoned us to follow her through the house as silently as possible.

As quiet as we were we made a certain amount of noise, and a man's voice from the room the girl had vacated called in German to know who was there.

131

The Germans outside heard him and going to the window told him they were hunting two Englanders they thought had gone through one of the houses. By this time we had reached the front door and the girl was quietly drawing the bolts.

"Goodbye, Engleesh boys." she whispered after she had opened it a crack and looked to see if the way was open for us.

I started with surprise to hear her use our language and paused to ask, "You are not French, then *Mademoiselle?*"

"*Oui, Monsieur*, but certainly I am French," she told me proudly. Then, at the look on my face, added with a wistful sigh, "But it is so hard to be patriotic and human, too, *n'est-ce pas?*"

I nodded, a look of sympathy perhaps, showing in my face. Poor kid, who was I to judge her. And I patted her thin shoulder over which her long hair hung loosely. Tears sprang into her eyes. Mine was probably the first understanding gesture anyone had given her for months. She raised her face to mine, her lips trembling, "Goodbye Engleesh boy." she said again.

The German we had heard in the bedroom was out in the kitchen opening the door for the others by now, calling as he did so. "Marie! Marie!" The Corporal was on the flags outside and looking back at me impatiently. Every second was priceless.

"Nice little bit o' fluff at that," commented the Corp, as we hurried down the dark and fortunately for us, deserted street.

"Oh, cheese it," I snapped, " and let's get outa here."

"Well, and who was holding up the parade while he got sentimental, I should like to know?"

Before I could answer a door opened behind us. I grabbed the Corp by the arm and we crouched down in the shadow of the houses. The voices at the door seemed to have come to some decision, for we heard it shut, and footsteps commenced to move cautiously down the stone flags toward us.

Leaping up, we hit off down the street as hard as we could go, crossing over to the other side as we did so. The noise of our break from cover was the signal for the German - there appeared to be only one - to shout at the top of his voice, *"Halt! Engländer!"*

As we knew he was unarmed or at the most had only a revolver we simply kept going, he, tearing along after us and shouting every few minutes. His cries brought answering shouts from the street by the canal and we could hear heavy boots pounding along down it running parallel with us.

At the first corner to the right we whipped around and noticed with relief that it was not cobbled like the road we had just left. Our feet made no sound on the soft earth. At the corner behind us our pursuer again called, *"Halt, Engländer!"*

We were leaving him behind, and it was a comfort to us to notice that the houses were getting farther apart. We were feeling the pace, however, and were blowing like whales, not being in any condition for a marathon race. Suddenly I saw a slight movement right ahead and before I could think of a thing to do, we were right in among a bunch of German officers.

They were as much surprised as we were and before they had grasped what was up, we were through them and on our way again. If the chap behind had only kept quiet, everything would have been all right. But just at the moment we broke free from the officers, he again shouted his, *"Halt, Engländer!"*

The officers at once tumbled to the cause of our unseemly haste and promptly joined the free-for-all. The Corp and I put on an extra burst as we passed them but we were nearly done, and it couldn't last. They were only a few yards behind us, fresh and in good condition for a pleasant and exciting little chase.

We tore along for another hundred yards or so when the nearest one, only a few yards in our rear, called to us, his voice sounding easy and careless and as if he could run a mile yet: "You had better halt, Tommee, one of my friends has a revolver and he might fire."

His voice sounded so cool and confident that we did as he suggested. We stopped. They were around us in an instant, and we saw that one of them had indeed a revolver although it was still in its holster.

"And what are you two doing here?" asked he of the cool voice and almost perfect English.

We could not get our breath for a moment which gave the old bean time to think of something to put them in a good humour, so when I could speak I told him we were hurrying to get home for Christmas. He grinned a little and told the others.

"Well," he said "come on back with us until we see what damage you have done around our village."

About this time our German with the voice had come up to us and observing the company he had suddenly barged into, stopped and tried to look at once military with his clicking heels and wire-sprung salute and yet very over-worked in his zeal to catch the runaways.

The officers were very proud of themselves and recounted with great enjoyment what was to them merely a pleasant incident. To us it was the end of our dearest hopes.

"Ah, well, better luck next time, Corp." I remarked, forgetting for the moment that one of our captors could speak English. The Corporal did not answer. I expect he was feeling pretty blue.

The German who had so successfully kicked over our applecart led the whole party back up into the town and to the house from which we had first fled. After hammering at the door until the German let us in we all filed into a sitting room off the main hall down which we had so recently stolen. Someone lit a candle which disclosed our host still wearing his pyjamas. He was a decent-looking sort and the others all addressed him as Heinrich so I gathered he, too, was an officer.

We were in for a tough bit of quizzing I knew and to tell a tale straight enough to sound convincing and yet not so as to drag in either the girl or our friend Victor, was going to be a job.

The others were having a pow-wow among themselves when the one who could speak English eyed me narrowly. He was a tall gangling bird with fair hair and a scrubby mustache. He was a little stoop-shouldered, too, like a farmer or student. His face reminded me of someone, but try as I would I could not get the connection. I suppose his nifty uniform and that German military air they all wear put me off the scent.

His blue eyes twinkled as he watched me. Presently he said: "Boom chika, ricka chicka."

"Rah, rah, rah!" I shot back with a laugh. In a flash memory had leaped back over four years of war and landed on the edge of a well trod and muddy football field...

"Schummerly!" He nodded, his eyes a little moist - as were mine - with emotion. We shook hands quietly in the self-conscious way men have when they are very glad indeed to meet someone. Dear old scientific Schum of all people! And a German officer at that! It was hard to imagine him being interested in infantry formations.

He was following the same line of thought. "Fancy you a soldier, Whiting! Why didn't you stay back with the snow and the wheat? And howeffer did you come to be a prisoner in our hands?"

"Well, you see, Shum," I explained with a grin, "we English aren't as good runners as you Germans." He laughed joyously, and the others turned at the sound and stared at us.

"*Wer ist es?*" asked one and Schummerly explained that I was an old acquaintance and class-mate of his peace-time days.

He was delighted to meet me, there was no doubt whatever of that. I could see he had a torrent of questions to ask me. I was a voice from his happy unmilitary past, and he wanted to hear the news I could give him. To me he was a rock in a weary land,

135

and I intended, if possible, to thoroughly exploit him. Not that I wasn't glad to see him for his own sake, but there were other reasons why I should not neglect to make a little hay while the sun was shining. To ensure that no suspicion could fall on our civvie friends, I gave Schum a carefully censored version of our adventures.

"Here," I said as I concluded, "can any of these others speak English?"

"I don't think so. Why?"

"How would it be if you suggested an adjournment till morning. Keep us under your own personal wing all night and give you and me a chance for a gabfest."

"H-mm," he demurred, "I doubt if the others would agree to that arrangement, but I'll try them." Schummerly then observed in his quiet voice that as it was getting late they should leave Heinrich to finish his dreams in peace and that the investigation of the prisoners could be left until morning. If it was satisfactory to them, he would be personally responsible for our safe-keeping over night.

After a little discussion the others agreed, and when we had bidden them goodnight in the street, Schummerly led us into a house three or four doors farther down.

"Carl! Carl! *hier kommen*," he called as we entered.

From a room off the hall came mumbled words followed by the sound of heavy feet thumping over the floor. A door opened and a bleary-eyed squarehead appeared holding a candle. He stood to attention in the doorway wearing only an alarmingly short shirt, his walrus mustache bristling fiercely as he saw us grinning at him. We did our noble best to keep from laughing aloud, while the poor fellow stood there blushing furiously. .

A woman's voice in another room down below called out to know the cause of the disturbance, and Schummerly told her he had two prisoners Anglais and would she like to get up and prepare them something to eat.

Feminine voices of eager compliance followed and our friend led the way upstairs to his room.

"Well." remarked our host as he shut the door and waved us to make ourselves at home, "I think the occasion calls for a small libation!"

Going to a cupboard he fished out a pot-bellied long-necked bottle of interesting appearance from which he poured all hands a generous tot. We raised our glasses and drank to Shum's toast: "Der Tag—of Peace!"

"And now, Whiting," said Shum, "if you will introduce me to your friend, we will talk." Apologizing for my negligence, I complied and the two shook hands warmly.

Just then a knock announced a visitor and in response to Schummerly's call the face of an elderly woman appeared around the door. "*Super est prêt en bas. Messieurs*," she announced.

"*Merci, Madame*," answered the captain, "My friends will be down for it at once."

Shum accompanied us down to the kitchen where our hostess had prepared a good meal of hot soup, fried eggs and plenty of bread and butter. After seeing us settled with our feet well under and our elbows firmly planted on the table he excused himself: "I think you fellows can get along without me for a while. The old lady looks as if she aching to ask you when the war'll be over. When you are finished come on up to the room."

"Strike me pink!" ejaculated the Corp, as we heard the German ascending the stairs, "if that chap is a Hun then I'm the Queen of Sheba! He goes security for us and leaves us sittin' here without even askin' for our blinkin' parole. Gorblimey, if I hadn't seen it myself I wouldn't have believed it, if St. Peter himself had told me!"

"Yeah," I agreed, grinning at his lapse into Wappingese, "weird fish, all of 'em. Some good, some bad, some rotten - just like we are - with the general

137

average panning out a fair to middling decency. And in the meantime, don't hog all that butter."

The Corp turned to Madame who was smilingly watching us enjoy our supper, "*Sale Boche?*" jerking his head in the direction Shum had taken.

"*Le Captaine? Non, Non. A German, oui, but a good German. Un bon garçon* - all the same a son to me."

The good soul then started on us. Were we newly captured? Escaped and recaptured! *Oh, là, là,* shaking her head in wonder . . . And the war, had we any news? The Germans give the civvies no news except of German victories. When did we think would come the end? Had the French suffered the frightful losses the Germans told of? Her two sons had departed with the retreating French army in '14, and she had no word from them since that day. One of them had left his wife and baby in this very town. The other, the younger, had been almost affianced to a young girl up the street but she, a thousand curses on her shameless head had been "amiable" to the Germans.

We glanced at one another, "Her name, Madame?"

"Marie Bouchoir!" We sipped our sugarless coffee in silence.

"*Ah, Messieurs, la guerre, la guerre, il est terrible, n'est-ce pas?* Never did it finish, Always the death, and the blood, and the tears . . ." We left her sitting by her lonely fireside, the heavy drops trickling down her worn cheeks.

Schummerly and I talked to a late hour of all the happenings that had befallen us since we had parted in the spring of '14. We talked of old classmates. He had been wounded twice, once before Verdun and the other opposite the Canadians at Passchendaele. He thought the next time would finish the job. Like myself he did not share the common fatalistic attitude expressed by the Tommies in the phrase "If your number's on a shell it'll get you." We both believed that if one kept returning to the front then sooner or later one would stop something serious. He hoped he would live it out if only for his parents' sake. His two brothers had been killed and his only sister, never very strong, had died of malnutrition.

We talked and talked. The Corporal had left us long before. When I had objected to using their clean bedding, Shum gave me a clean suit of his underwear and begged another suit for the Corp from Madame which she had laid by for her own men folk when and if they returned. Well washed, in clean clothes and with our uniforms being cooked in the local delouser while we slept, our little trip promised us some compensations at any rate.

It must have been three or four in the morning before I crept quietly in beside the Corp who was ripping off the cordwood in great style. He didn't bother me, however, and it was not long before I had hold of the other handle of his saw if we could believe Shum's report in the morning.

Our outer garments were a little late coming back from the delouser, or whatever the Germans called that institution of wholesale slaughter, and we had to attend breakfast in Shum's room clad only in our borrowed undies. We borrowed his shaving kit and by the time we climbed into our no longer lively uniforms we felt and doubtless looked new men.

After breakfast Schummerly went out to learn what was to be done about us, leaving our old friend, Herr Short-shirt on guard at the door in full military regalia, spiked helmet and all.

Presently Shum returned. "You are to be returned to Fresnes this afternoon, going as far as Valenciennes by train."

We all exchanged gloomy looks, but we sat and smoked and gassed away until about ten o'clock when Schum had to go on parade. In the meantime we had bribed Short-shirt to rustle us four loaves of bread and a small tin of butter. While we were gloating over these Madame came to the door and timidly offered us a small sack of potatoes and a piece of raw salt horse.

Our gratitude for the munificence of her gift was

139

such that we could do little more than blurt out our thanks. In fact we hesitated to take it not knowing how she was fixed for supplies for herself. But Schummerly, coming in just then, assured us that she could spare what she had offered without hardship to herself.

"How about these loaves, then?" asked the Corp. "Your man hunted 'em up. Did he rob your private larder?"

"I think not," grinned the officer. "There is a ration dump around the corner and - oh well, you know."

The three of us had another hour or two together, then two tall Prussians - Kaiser's Body Guards, or some such regiment, took us over and escorted us to the station. Shum came along and shook hands with us there on the platform much to the shocked surprise of several other officers who happened to be passing.

Chapter Eleven

About dusk we arrived at Valenciennes. We were lined up with fifteen or twenty newly-captured prisoners also bound for the prison-lager at Fresnes. At the sight, a brilliant idea occurred to our two Prussians. Why not hand the Corp and me over to the guards in charge of the larger party and save themselves the long walk to Fresnes and back? The chance of a night in Valenciennes was not to be lightly disregarded.

While our guards were arranging this with the others, the Corp nudged me and whispered, "When I have my night marching to do I always like to get in the centre of the column, don't you?"

I started . . . Why not? The nights were still dark. We had ample food to last a week and we were due for a week of punishment anyway.

"We-ell, I don't know," I muttered. Then we squeezed into the line-up at what we judged was the most strategic point. After seeing that we were already under the wings of our new guards, the Prussians left, looking well pleased with themselves. Then the word was given and the party led off - from the wrong end!

"Oh, I'll bet!" remarked the Corp disgustedly.

"Minor troubles, old egg. Minor troubles." I chided.

By the time we had left Valenciennes behind us, it was quite dark, and we had gradually worked our way up the column to within a few files of the lead guard. Occasionally wagons or lorries rumbled by.

Then up loomed a train of horse-drawn ambulances proceeding at a walking pace heading back for the town, the iron-shod hoofs and wheels making a great clattering. The Corp nodded towards the passing vehicles. "Behind one of these?" Furtively I glanced about. A guard who had been walking by the side of the column a little way in our rear had temporarily disappeared. Chances seemed excellent.

"Righto! The next if you like."

Over my shoulder I spoke to the two men in the file behind us. "Keep closed up, please, and don't burst into song if anyone enquires for us." They stared at me uncomprehendingly - probably thinking I was a bit cracked.

"Come on!" growled the Corp jerking my arm.

Giving a hand-waggle of farewell to the Britishers, I followed the Corp as he left the ranks, and we about-faced behind the ambulance wagon. At that instant my heart gave a leap. Two Germans were seated on the rear end of the wagon! Moreover as we turned about I glimpsed the flanking guard as he re-appeared through the prisoner files. Had he seen us?

Without a word we brushed by the knees of the two seated Germans who stared at us in surprise. A moment later we were hidden from their sight by the following team.

"Halt!" came a roar from behind us. At the order not only the prisoners but as many of the ambulances as were within hearing stopped and precipitately we fled across the road, through a ditch and brought up sharp against a thickset hedge of hawthorn. It seemed impenetrable, being stoutly reinforced with stakes driven well into the ground.

From the double column on the road came shouted orders and then the clatter of running feet as they converged upon us. We threw over our food parcels and tore frantically at the prickly barrier.

"You first," I gasped as we snatched out a small gap. "You're smallest."

He leaped headlong and crashed half way through. I shoved and he tugged . . . Something gave with a rip, and he was free. On his heels I dived into the thorns, just as the nearer of the Germans scrambled down the ditch.

"*Halt, du!*" he ordered. I felt some obstruction catch me over the hips.

"*Ganz gut,*" I said in a resigned tone, while to the Corp I muttered: "Grab me by the pants and lift for godsake!" He suddenly hauled like a hero, and with a desperate kick and a heave I popped through the hole like a pip out of a lemon. As I scrambled to my feet my arm struck a bundle. Grub! I swooped it up, and we went from there as hard as we could leg it across the plowed field in which we found ourselves.

Half an hour later when we had shaken off our pursuers, we sank to rest in some long grass beside a railway grade, our lungs sobbing.

"What a life!" panted the Corp after a little. "Where do we go from here and how do we get there?"

"Well," I returned, "if there is anything upon which you desire full information, just enquire at the wicket."

"I'd like the address of a good tailor," grumbled the Corp, viewing his ruined trousers. "Haven't got a safety pin have you?"

We lay for a time discussing the situation; whether to hit west for the line or north to Holland was the problem. While we were still undecided, a freight train from Vallenciennes came puffing slowly along. The opportunity was not to be ignored.

"In any case," I said picking up the bundle of food and jumping to my feet, "Let's get out of the district before morning." We leaped for the hand-grips on the passing car and a moment later lay together on the swaying roof.

"What say we have a slice or two of old Carl's bread?" suggested the Corp after a time. "I feel as if I'd like to restore a tissue or two."

Presently the train picked up speed and rumbled along at a good rate, soon getting into the Raismes forest area through which we were travelling when the Kid was shot. I thought I recognized the very group of buildings that had diverted us from our path and caused us to encounter the sentry who had killed him.

When, a little later, we roared over the bridge crossing a canal, I heaved a sigh of relief. There would not likely be any definite search beyond that natural barrier.

Hour after hour, mile after mile, the train carried us on. At first I could tell by the stars that we were going north-west, then the sky clouded and a slow rain began so that I lost my sense of our whereabouts. The train halted frequently for varying periods in darkened towns during which we lay flat and motionless. We began to feel chilled after our lengthy heat across the fields. The increasing drizzle of rain added to our discomfort.

"Brrr-rh," presently burst from the Corp "If we stay here a minute longer I'll die on the spot. Let's go for a walk and p'raps we'll find a more sheltered corner."

I peered over the edge to the next car as it bumped and swayed along. "Have a heart," I begged. "It's all I can do to hang on here."

"Rats!" and he hopped up and jumped across the gap with no effort whatever and ran down the train towards the engine as calmly as if he had been running along one of his London pavements. Presently he came skipping back. "There's an open coal-truck up in front." he said. "We can dig down into that an' get a bit of shelter." Grabbing me by the arm he hauled me to my feet, groaning and protesting with stiffness from the cold and wet.

"Buck up," he urged. "You're as safe as a church.

144

What's all the fuss about?" The train lurched and bounced about alarmingly as it roared on through the night, but after a little my companion's confidence to some extent communicated itself to me, and I followed him timorously over the inky voids between the cars. Gaining the coal-truck, the Corp busied himself digging in the most sheltered side, heaving the huge lumps overboard despite my shocked objections.

"Garn," he snorted, "This'll help us win the war! It's Jerry's coal, isn't it? The Belgian farmers'll find it, won't they? And we've got to get warm somehow, don't we? Well, then, lend a hand."

We soon had a fairly snug retreat, and though I can't honestly recommend a hole in a pile of coal as comfortable resting place, the fact remains that in spite of our cramped limbs and wet cold bodies, we did snatch a few cat-naps during the night.

Toward morning we gave thought to the business of leaving the train. Whether to wait until the train stopped and take a chance of being nabbed, or jump and risk a broken neck or leg. A little later the engine whistled for a bridge, and peering over the edge of our truck I perceived a dim line of trees in a valley just ahead. At the same instant I noticed dawn was paling the eastern sky.

"Tell you what," I said rising, "there'll be a canal here. Let's leave on the embankment on the other side of it. We'll have the bank to roll down - it'll break our fall and the roar of the train will cover any noise."

"Sounds all right, if it works all right," conceded the Corp. The train rumbled over the bridge and I kept a sharp lookout for the sentry or his box. Neither was visible from our side.

"Let's go!" We clambered over the edge to tumble head over heels down a steep bank, coming to rest with a loud double splash in a ditch at the bottom. While we were rallying our scattered wits and digging the weeds and slime from our eyes, the train disappeared.

145

My head rang from a crack I had received en route to the ditch, and for a moment my caution was relaxed. I splashed and floundered toward the bank and good old terra firma.

A sharp "*Wer da?*" from above us on the railway brought me back to realities with a jar. A little way along the ditch I could see my companion crouching in the water peering up at the sentry who stood looking down at us. We could see him plainly against the lightening sky, but I doubt if he could see us.

"*Wer da?*" again came the challenge.

I was pretty sure he had not seen us leave the train, therefore he would not be sure that the sounds he heard were being made by men. They might be an animal. To put his mind at rest and to dissuade him from calling out the rest of the guard or opening fire on us, I boldly scrambled up the bank on all fours, grunting hugely like a large well-fed porker. The Corp promptly followed this excellent example.

Over my shoulder I could see the black silhouette of the sentry as he pondered this development. Then to our horrified surprise he shouted joyously: "*Emil! Franz!* Come quick! Free *schwein-fleisch!* Bring a knife!" We waited neither for Emil, Franz or the knife to take up the trail of the lonesome swine but scampered into the shelter of some bushes and from there across several small fields as fast as our little trotters could take us.

We heard no sound of pursuit and soon slackened our speed. Our most pressing need of the moment was cover for the day, but apparently the only bush or scrub of any sort was back at the railway bridge, and that was out of the question. Besides, and I groaned with dismay to think of it, I had dropped our sack of potatoes somewhere between the train and the ditch, so that we were now without food.

Soon we came to a hard road and followed it for a time in case the *schwein-fleisch* hunters tried to follow our tracks. Houses and small villages were growing visible and we finally came to rest in a field of

beans. These were in stooks two and a half feet high.
"Bed and board for the day, old chappie," I remarked with a grateful sigh.

"Where?" asked the Corp.

"Right here," I told him, grasping a couple of bundles and dropping them flat on the ground. "Carry in a few of these sheaves from that other row and we'll have a home in two flaps of a bee's wing." We soon had a warm, fairly dry bed of bean stalks hedged about and over with more bundles.

"What, ho!" cried the Corporal, as he ran up with his last armful. "Look what I've found," and he threw into our bivouac a huge turnip. "It was growing all by its lonesome over there."

"Actually, of course," I said, crawling in beside him, "There is something in what you say, but I have it on excellent authority that any plant out of place is a weed. A turnip in a bean-field is most certainly out of place, therefore it is a weed."

After breakfasting on turnip and shelled beans, we removed our boots and wet socks. The latter we placed under our bodies to dry, the boots just inside the bivvy. The day was none too warm. A raw wind searched through our meagre shelter and awakened us a-shiver after two or three hours of fitful sleep. Fortunately the rain of the night before had ceased. For a long time we lay and talked of our chances. Finally we dropped to sleep.

Suddenly I opened my eyes. Wide. My heart a-pound. I could hear a gentle flick-flickering growing fainter. I peeped cautiously around the sheaf by my head.

A German! But he was walking away rapidly carrying something in his hands. "Corp!" I whispered, "Corp!" I had to shake him hard to awaken him. "A Jerry just went by here!"

"Eh, a Jerry? By here?" he echoed stupidly.

"Good lord, d'you think he saw us?"

"Oh, no, he'd have pinched us if he had. We're quite safe."

"Well, I don't know about that. We'd better get our boots on and be ready to make a dash for it if need be." And he reached for his foot-gear.

"Great Scott! They're gone! Gone!"

"Who's gone?"

"Our boots!" I jerked to a sitting position ignoring the fact that half of our shelter fell down as I did so.

Too true! The German had carried them off. He had come right up to our bivvy, recognized us as Britishers, and probably being unarmed, had taken our boots to prevent our escape while he had gone for help to arrest us. And the two of us lying right under his nose dead to the world.

We stared bleakly at each other. The Corp was the first to make a move. "Come on! Let's run for it," he urged. "We aren't caught yet."

"Without boots?" I shook my head. "Too hard on the old daisy roots, old top. Our feet would be ribbons in no time."

Gloomily I watched the German disappear among a group of buildings a half mile or so distant. Soon he would be coming back followed by all hands to see the fun. But would he trouble to bring those boots back again? . . . It was worth investigating!

"Follow old Leather-stocking," I said as, crouching low, I ran off at right angles to the route the German had taken. The Corp followed after picking up our socks and cramming them into his pocket.

As I expected, at the edge of the field was a shallow ditch bordered on either side with tall grass. Into this we jumped and, still keeping low, headed now toward the group of buildings from which a moment later we saw a stream of grey-clad figures emerge and run in a straggling mob in the direction of our late shelter. Putting on speed we cut in behind them and utilizing what little cover we could find, soon arrived at the outskirts of the farm which seemed deserted. Here we stopped for a brief council of war.

"Chances are that Jerry dropped his load of boots somewhere near the door of whichever building his crowd is billeted in," I told the Corp. "A hundred to one everyone has gone off hunting us. If we do meet up with someone he'll most likely be Belgian and not to be feared. If you look around the house I'll search the barn."

We ran across the open street swiftly, our bare feet making no sound upon the cobbles. Then we separated. A moment later I peeped inside a barn door; no boots there. A heavy cart-horse stood in a stall and beyond him a ladder into the loft above. I was just wondering if there was a chance the German had taken them up there when the Corp rushed to the barn, our precious footwear in his hands.

"Here, quick!" he panted as he raced by "An officer in the house saw me!"

I snatched at the boots. At top speed we hit for the open fields. The sun was low, and I knew if we could only elude them for another half hour or so, our chances were yet good. Then, glancing back, we saw a figure leave the buildings on horseback. No trees, not even a ditch was in sight, and the officer was lashing his mount at a gallop towards us.

"Those hops!" cried the Corp dashing off toward a plantation that stood fully two hundred yards away. I panted after him, though with little hope that we could gain shelter before the officer caught up with us. Puffing and gasping we plunged into the sanctuary of the tall vines. Withered and sparse as they climbed their long strings toward the high over-hanging wires they offered us the best protection in miles. We were leading the race by twenty-five yards when we dived into one of the long aisles and ran toward the opposite end.

A revolver cracked and a bullet zipped overhead. We promptly dodged through the hops into another row. The officer also attempted to cut through, but the horse balked, and though we could hear the rider swearing and thumping his mount, pursuit was at a temporary stand-still. Then we heard several shots.

"Signals for help, I expect," panted the Corp. "Let's

get our boots on while we get a breather. My feet are almost done."

"Mine, too," I agreed. Sitting down we pulled on our foot-gear and mighty good it felt. While we hurriedly laced our boots, a rather ominous silence had taken the place of the previous uproar between the officer and his horse.

"What do you suppose that bounder is up to?" whispered the Corp as he rose to his feet. For answer, there came to our ears a slight rustling in the hops a few yards behind us.

"He's hitched his horse and is stalking us. Come on!" I hissed. As silently as possible we ran down the row. A large bunch of hops had broken loose from the overhanging wires and now lay in a ragged heap. Behind this we hid. Presently we heard a slight rustling in the hops several rows over from us. The sounds came abreast; went beyond us.

After a time darkness settled over the level fields and we felt fairly safe. We worked our way to the margin of a canal where we sat for a well-earned rest and a council-of-war. For one thing we wanted to know where we were before going any farther. Another, was the pressing, or rather gnawing question of food. Since our rather sketchy breakfast of turnip and beans in the morning, we had eaten nothing all day.

"If we can spot a civvy," mused the Corp chewing on a spear of grass, "we can hit him up for some grub and find out where we are." We stared about but no civvies conveniently appeared.

"The next best thing," I suggested, "is to hunt up another bean field. We can at least . . ." I broke off, listening. "What'n heck's that?" To our ears came a steady chug-chug-chug of an engine.

"Barges!" said the Corp. The steady noise approached and drew abreast. We could hear the well-known gentle lap-lap of the water against the prows on the other side of the embankment.

I lay outstretched, gazing up at the peeping stars,

while the Corp, always interested in shipping, craned his head above the fringe of protecting grasses and watched the passing barges.

"I say!" he whispered down to me, "these fellows are carrying down old iron the same as our lot." I rolled over and heaved myself up beside him. "There's four of them, too. Great Scott, man! They're the same! That's Victor's tow as sure as shooting." He hissed excitedly, pointing forward. "There's the same old reaping-machine we hid under!"

"Mower," I corrected.

"Oh, what's the difference? Wonder if our hole is still unoccupied?" said the Corp with a homesick sigh.

"Wouldn't be a bit surprised. Want to go back?"

"A few days' rest wouldn't come amiss after all these hare-an'-hound cross-country runs, but I expect Victor thinks he is well rid of us."

"Anyhow, we have to get some grub. My stomach thinks my throat's cut."

As the barges disappeared into the darkness we sat up. "First thing," I said, "let's get our bearings and decide where we'll head for. Those barges are going north. We're on the east side of the canal. North of us is Holland and the sea. West and south of us is the front line. Now, where are we going?"

"You had rotten luck on the front line, so let's have a try to the north. Yo-ho! The briny deep for me," said the Corp."

"All right," I agreed, and we struck out. Before long we came to a bean field where we stopped and appeased our hunger.

Footsteps approached and we lay watching in the direction of the sound. A figure loomed up on our side of the road carrying a large bundle of withes. By his dress, the man was a peasant.

"He's a civvy, let's ask him, shall we?"

"Righto!"

"*Monsieur! Monsieur!*" I called gently, still keeping low.

The man paused. "*Ja?*" he answered.

151

"Parlez-vous français?" I repeated my question.

"Vlaamsch!" he returned.

"Flemish! I might have known it." I grumbled. "Still, it's much like German. Ask him in *Deutsch* the name of the nearest town."

"Termonde," answered the peasant to the question.

"Is it a big town?" asked the Corp.

"Very, very big!"

"How far Antwerp?" He didn't know - maybe fifty, sixty kilometres.

"Which direction?" The man pointed to the northeast.

"Danke schön." The peasant plodded on.

"That's why they were running so late. Though for that matter they must have been doing a lot of late running to get as far as this since we saw them last."

"Which isn't such a long time ago," I grinned.

"Lumme! that's right, too, though it seems weeks since." The corporal returned to his apparently rambling soliloquy. "Those chaps on the barges 'll be wanting some shut-eye," he went on. "They'll figure on the M. P.'s doing the guarding." He paused and after a little, grinned at me. "How abaht it?" I knew what was in the beggar's mind all right.

"Oh, Lord," I groaned, "We'll have a devil of a time following those crafts up into the town and getting aboard again."

"Well, but mark this. We've got to look sharp and get well out of this district after all the hullabaloo we kicked up this afternoon. There's probably search parties out looking for us now. And they'll comb the whole countryside tomorrow."

"Guess you're right there," I conceded.

"And another thing," went on the Corp. "From now on, the country lies pretty low. That means canals. Canals mean bridges and bridges mean guards. How abaht it?"

"Oh, all right ," I said at length, "we can't foozle it much worse than we did this afternoon."

We crammed our pockets full of beans until we

had enough to last us for another three days or more. By this time it was getting latish - eleven or so and civilian traffic was at an end. Anyone we encountered now was almost certain to be a German. The old houses by the canal gave way to a street that, dim and echoing, stretched endless beside the dark water. Our boots made considerable noise so we stopped and took them off, thereafter stealing forward in almost complete silence.

Then came a steady tramp, tramp, tramp from behind us. A patrol! We scuttled ahead for a little, then ducked into the shelter of a dark archway, hiding down behind the heavy door while the patrol clumped past.

"In their rear," whispered the Corp twitching my sleeve. And, cautiously emerging, we stole along some hundred yards or so, behind them.

We soon came abreast of some barges tied up and silent for the night, but they were not those we sought, and we crept along farther down into the town. The buildings were taller. We were both feeling the strain when opposite some more barges the Corp caught my arm. "Here we are!" he whispered.

Stealthily approaching the barge that had given us sanctuary before, we craned and listened, every nerve tense. All seemed exactly the same and we crept quietly aboard and wriggled down into our old corner. We did not dare break the silence by talking and spent the rest of the long night in fitful and uncomfortable slumber, being frequently awakened by the passing patrol and the ache in our cramped limbs.

Shortly after the chill dawn streaked through to us, we heard the engine of the leading barge start up and felt the gentle tug as it took up the load.

"And off we goes again!" crowed the Corp in a guarded voice. His jubilation was short-lived. The sound of water under our prow died away very shortly after we had started.

"Tied up in a fresh berth," croaked my companion. "Now what?"

We couldn't guess and daren't investigate. All day we lay there surrounded by countless water-front noises. At night the sounds died down and we crept out to lie along the bulwark, stealthily dipping our hands down to the water below us to quench our thirst with a few drops that tasted like stale dishwater. We finally crept back to our hiding place.

In the morning the engine again started and this time it kept on. After a time the noises of the tow faded and only the water sounds and that of the engine came to us. Lap-lap, lap-lap; hour after hour. Only an occasional long pause that may have been a lock checked our steady progress.

We beguiled away the weary hours by yarning about what we would be doing in the near future if our luck held for a few days more. The Corp said he would likely join the merchant marine after he had had a few weeks' holiday.

"Thank God!" he averred fervently. "They don't send us back to the trenches if we escape from prison camp."

"Well," I said emphatically, "I'm going on a bust. At least a week in London, and longer if the money lasts. What a time I'll have! Clean sheets and pyjamas and fish and chips! Slathers of girl shows and good thick juicy steaks and two fat kippers every morning for breakfast!"

"As for me," said the Corp "I know of a little shop on a side street in Hounslow where you can get a jolly fine blow-out of tripe and onions, coffee and a whacking big issue of bread and butter for a shilling." We were off, eating our way around the Empire.

Chapter Twelve

All that day and night the barges glided steadily on. About four in the afternoon of the second day after leaving Termonde, we came to what sounded like a large town. After a number of stops and starts we came to rest beside a wharf where we could hear trains moving up and down at frequent intervals.

"If this ain't Antwerp, I'm barmy." announced the Corp.

The rhythmic tread of marching feet approached; halted just beyond us. Then men clambered onto the barges and as we could tell by the clanking metal, began to unload them. The Corp and I looked at one another with faces pale through our grime. Heavy feet thumped on the peak over our heads. The men commenced heaving and tugging at the work of unloading. Bang! Clank! Crash! Clang! With the disappearance of each piece of junk the light in our retreat grew stronger and our hearts sank lower.

For ten minutes not a word did the labourers utter, then suddenly the one working nearest us said to his mate, "Hi, Bew, wot die's this?"

"Sunday, I finks," murmured Bew.

"Gordstrewth! Sunday, aye! My ol' woman'll be just abaht puttin' the kettle on f'r cup o' tea, I expects.

An' 'en arterwards she'll be dressin' up in 'er Sunday gow-ter-meetin's and poppin' orf ter church."

My relief at hearing the mother tongue was so great that I was on the point of scrambling out, believing that in some strange way we had reached safety. However, before I could make a move, the Corp grabbed my arm and whispered: "Hey, quiet, you silly chump. They're only prisoners." I settled back reluctantly, regaining my mental bearings.

We crouched lower and lower in our corner, as piece after piece was removed from the barge. When discovery was only a matter of minutes, the Corp said in a casual conversation tone: "I say, old chap, don't take any more from this end of if you can help it." The man nearest us jumped and wheeled around.

"Eh? What?" he blurted, staring down into our corner.

"Carry on," said the Corp "We're only two escaping prisoners. Don't make a fuss or you'll bring the Jerries around."

"Escyping pris'ners! Lumme! But you cawn't escype any farther. We've got to unload these barges and then you'll be caught y'knaow."

"Hang it all, man, you don't have to work all night, do you?"

"Naow, but . . ."

"Well then, go easy on this end of the barge and give us a chance. You'll be knocking off presently. What place is this?"

"Antwerp. Are you gowin' to have a try at gettin' into Holland?"

"Something of that sorts, p'raps. But you'd better be banging something around or you'll have a Jerry after us."

The news of our presence spread among the other workers and one by one they made the occasion to work towards our corner and peer in at us like small boys looking at a couple of monkeys in a cage.

"Buzz off!" the Corp entreated finally. "None of you chaps have paid your sixpence."

156

They were very good. Soldiered on the job as much as possible until only a few bunches of stuff lay between us and the open floor of the barge. Then about dusk they were ordered ashore, lined up, numbered and marched off.

The night closed down. Engines whistled and shunted back and forth. Pedestrians were few and those few appeared to have business.

"And now what?" I asked as we stood looking over the side of the barge. "From now on you are the master of my fate - the captain of my what-is-it. When does the next boat leave for Blighty, officer?"

"Well," he answered, "I wouldn't mind betting a brass farden that we're fenced in here in some way. Notice there's no women or kids about? Sure as Old Nick, our next move will have to be a cautious one."

After a bit he added, "I think our best chance of getting out of the town is while people are still moving about." I nodded and we scrambled up onto the deserted wharf.

"Where's all the shipping?" I asked. "I thought Antwerp was a seaport."

"So it is, sort of. But there's nothing much as far down as this. All the big boats are docked the other side of the town. We've got to head back to the southward and circle the town in order to get past all that . . . Here, duck, quick!"

We went to cover behind a pile of old uniforms and iron junk as the head of a small column appeared. As they went past us we could see two Germans in front carrying rifles with bayonets fixed. Another prisoner fatigue party.

"What say we shoulder into this parade until we get outside the dockyards?" whispered the Corp.

"Too risky," I hissed back. "For all we know they are billeted down here somewhere and we mightn't have a chance to break away again."

"Well then, how about falling in behind them like we did the patrol in Termonde. We'll at least find the way out o' here."

157

"Okay, then."

After the last of the column had gone past us we arose and walked quietly along in their rear.

"Jerries coming!" suddenly grunted the Corp nodding towards the front. We both halted before a flat pile of corrugated iron sheets. There was no cover or shelter in sight.

"Here," I said, "get busy. You're on fatigue!" And I lifted a huge sheet on my back and bowing under the burden walked steadily towards the oncoming Germans. The Corp had followed my example and was right behind me. The two Jerries passed us with only a casual glance.

"Better try and hold this job," whispered the Corp. I grunted agreement.

The prisoner party ahead suddenly disappeared through a gateway in a high boarded wall. No sentry was in sight so we boldly advanced and stepped through when . . .

"*Halt!*" A sentry appeared from behind the barrier and pointed his rifle directly at my stomach.

I stood there dumbly, my piece of sheet-iron still held over my bowed shoulders, the old mental gears for the moment refusing to mesh.

"Got a light, comrade?" asked the Corp in his execrable Tommee-Deutsch, coolly fishing out a seldom-used pipe.

The German lowered his rifle hesitatingly.

"*Haben Sie Feuer?*" asked my companion again.

The German mumbled something and commenced to feel in his pocket. He could see, of course, that we were British, so I took my cue from the Corporal and asked boldly. "*Gefangennens vorwartz?*" - pointing in the direction we had seen the column disappear.

"*Gefangennes, ja.*"

"*Danke schön,*" and the restraining influence of the bayonet having been removed from my immediate midst I strode forward.

When we were safely out of hearing - "What a nerve!" I exploded in a gust of awed admiration.

158

"Yes," puffing on the pipe, "it was a bit cheeky of him to stop two hard-working Britishers like us. I've a good mind to write to his officer. Doocid cheeky, I calls it." Gratefully leaving the menace of the guarded dockyards we continued steadily along the road by the waterside and presently saw the prisoner column turn right down a side street.

We passed a few civilians, but they hardly glanced at us as we marched steadily along under our protecting sheets. Once an officer paused and seemed on the point of saying something, but we did not falter. After eyeing us doubtfully for a moment he went on his way evidently reassured by our honest hard-working appearance.At last we came to some open fields on the south side of the town and in a ditch we discarded our tinware with a hearty clank.

When we came out on the Scheldt many sea-going craft, apparently devoid of life, lay to anchor near the shore. The channel was empty. The Corp peered at the dark water intently. "The tide's going out now. We've no time to waste," and he led the way quietly along, eyeing each vessel carefully.

"Who owns all these boats anyway, Corp? Won't it be stealing if we make off with one of them?"

"Stealing? Nah!" scoffed he scornfully. "Most of 'em's owned or been commandeered by the Jerries. If one is missing at the end of the war, it'll be charged up to the side that loses."

He paused opposite a fishing smack that lay heeled over fairly close to the shore. To it was attached a light skiff that swung with the tide.

"Let's try this," he whispered, leading the way boldly into the mud. I shrank back for an instant. "Come on!" he urged. "We haven't time to take our things off."

I followed him, sinking to the knees at the first step. We plunged forward. The water rose to my waist; to my chest. Ahead of me the Corporal was swimming and as the water reached my chin I saw him pull himself over the side of the boat. I kicked off, paddling frantically but my heavy boots and clothes pulled me down. I had gained only a few yards when I felt my strength ebbing and my strokes grow feeble. I kicked and splashed desperately, but the water ran into my mouth, hissed in my ears and flowed over my head. Suddenly I didn't care.

The next thing I felt was a horrible pain in my arm. The Corp had it over the edge of the boat and was trying to drag me in. I was about done, but the little chap heaved and tugged manfully while I helped feebly so that at last he got me over, and I lay on the bottom gasping and choking. Without wasting any further time on me he untied the skiff and pushed off into the current with a long pole that lay across the seats.

Presently I sat up and the Corp grinned down at me. "Near go, that! I looked around and you had vanished so I pushed the boat over to where I saw some bubbles. How you feeling?"

"Rotten!" I told him, my teeth chattering so that I could hardly frame the word.

He stood up and beat his arms vigorously about his body, then knelt beside me and rubbed a little life into my hands and legs. When I was able to do that for myself he pulled up a seat-board and using that for a paddle sent the dinghy forward into the stream and continued using it to increase our speed.

"Lend us a hand with the pole as soon as you can, old chap," he said over his shoulder.

"Aye-aye, Cap'n," I answered with a flicker of cheer. On the banks black masses of buildings and the nearer cluster of spidery masts tapering into the starlight glided silently behind us.

"Last time I was up here," commented the Corp, "this place swarmed with craft. We seem to be the only ones alive tonight."

"How much farther?" I asked after we had paddled steadily for two good hours.

"Getting jolly close now, I think. As near as I remember it, Holland is about ten miles from Antwerp.

160

We walked three miles or more past the town before we got the boat, so at that rate . . ."

A dazzling beam of light shot across the water ahead. It paused, then swung downstream, paused again, then back towards us, as we floated steadily onward. The powerful ray swept past leaving us blinded; returned and rested pitilessly on our tiny craft. We sat there staring into the overpowering glare as if hypnotized.

"We're done," said the Corp dully, dropping his makeshift paddle inboard.

From the water-edge a motor roared into life, and a black shape swept towards us. The roar died to a gentle murmur, and a boat-hook fastened onto our bow as the motor boat glided past.

"Who are you?" demanded a voice in German. Neither of us answered. Then in English, "Are you escaping prisoners?"

"Yes," growled the Corp.

A rope whirled through the air and fell into the boat. "I thought so. Bend that line through your ring-bolt. You are re-captured."

Five minutes later we were drinking coffee before a hot stove, our wet clothes a-steam. Our captors, river police, did not immediately consign us to a cell but noticing our wet and bedraggled condition allowed us to get comfortably warm in their own billet. One brought us some ration bread, and how we did enjoy the sour brown stuff! Another gave us a cigar each.

He of the nautical English was the sergeant - tall and blonde and educated in England. He asked us from what lager we had escaped and was immensely interested in the sketchy outline we gave him of our adventures. Needless to say we made no mention of the barge.

When we were fairly warm and dry we were locked in a comfortable cell opening off the common room of the police billets. On the floor were several straw palliasses and two or three blankets.

161

"Well," said the Corp as he wrung out a sock, "We ain't got much money but we had a lotta fun, eh?"

I was busy examining the window fastenings when he spoke. Outside the glass I could see stout bars set in concrete.

As day broke we were awakened by one of our jailers bringing in some breakfast of coffee and bread. An hour or so later two elderly Germans appeared, one very tall and thin, the other very short and fat.

"Come, Tommee," said the short fat one, "undt don't try any fonnee stoff or ve vill blow der hell oudt off you." He waggled his rifle and grinned at us very amiably. The tall thin one eyed us gloomily as if he just knew something unpleasant would happen shortly. His forecast, if he actually made one, was way out. A very pleasant time was had by all - at least until after the wanderers had been returned. They escorted us by train back to Fresnes.

The short fat one whom the Corp christened "Willie' had been a steward on board a freighter plying between Antwerp and New York and he and the little Cockney found a lot in common. When we showed no signs of springing any "fonnee stoff" they released their iron discipline and obligingly looked the other way when fellow civilian passengers showed signs of wanting to give away some food and tobacco.

Of war news we learned that the Americans had made some gains. "But," scoffed Willie, waving an arm, "Dot iss nossing. Ve haff der Russkies finished; der Serbians; undt der Roumanians alles finished."

"Italy." put in the tall thin one whom the Corp called Tim.

"Ja, undt Italy iss finished too!" shouted Willie excitedly, waving his other arm. "Ve finish France undt Englandt and America by next sommer, Ja!"

Tim wasn't so sure. He thought the war never would end. Not for another year.

We smoked and argued and ragged one another companionably whiling away the long hours of the journey. We had to change several times and that

162

night we spent in the city lockup in Brussels. Quite a comfortable jail as jails go and the Corp and I enjoyed the first real sleep we had had for what seemed like aeons.

About ten the next morning Willie and Tim took us in charge again, and we caught the train for Vallenciennes where we arrived about three in the afternoon.

The last hour or so of the journey, marching from Vallenciennes to Fresnes, the hitherto sparkling quip and rally of two members of our party suffered a decided slump. A leaden depression set in which made cheerful conversation a toilsome burden. The nearer we drew to Fresnes the fewer and feebler grew the wisecracks.

Outside the prison Willie paused. "Gootby, poys," he said, his pudgy hand that looked like a bunch of bananas, outstretched. "Goot luck!" We shook hands, grinned at them with a forced cheerfulness and marched between them through the outer gate.

At the orderly room we were at once invited inside to meet our old friend Hindenburg. Willie and Tim disappeared. The Kommandant was in his usual hostile mood and on getting the glad tidings of our safe return steamed into action without delay.

At his first salvo of horribly fulminating Teutonic curses we lowered our colours in unconditional surrender, bowing our heads to the storm and letting him work off his peevishness in volleys and thunders, while we tried to convey by our expressions that we had not intended to cause him annoyance.

The barrage roared and crashed about us culminating in a tremendous broadside of everything he had. Charging us towards the door he shoved us through it and helped us down the steps with a well placed number twelve each that shook me, as the Corp might have expressed it, from top-mast to bilge-scuppers.

"Lordy," I growled, rubbing my damaged lower works as we were led off to our private cell, "I would sure like to get that bird where I could bust him on the beezer for a day or two."

"Chuck it!" replied the Corp. "Be a sport. You can hardly expect him to kiss you. If too many of us get away, he'll lose his cushy job and p'raps find himself back in the trenches. You've had your fun, now pay your price like a little man. Anyway, he hasn't started on us yet. Wait until tomorrow night and you'll have had some cause to grouse."

"You're a cheerful little playmate all right. What's he going to do to us then? I hardly understood a word he said."

"Well, half rations for a start, pack drill at the trot, solitary confinement in the dog-kennels and one or two other little things I didn't quite catch myself." I groaned to hear him. Still, as he said, we had had our fun and it was up to us to pay the piper.

We slept very little that night as there were no mattresses, blankets or a single thing to keep us off the cold cement floor. In one of the corners we huddled down together, our heads pillowed on our arms and shivered the night away.

Next morning for breakfast we received a piece of bread about the size of two fingers, a drink of cold water and that was all. We had no sooner eaten it than we had visitors in the persons of the camp sergeant, Cohen, the interpreter and an extra guard.

Come on, Corporal," said Cohen, "you have to fall in right away. Orders came in last night for all NCO's to be moved to Germany."

The Corp and I stared at one another in dismay. This would mean parting. We might never see one another again,

"*Kommen, 'raus!*" snarled the sergeant.

Ignoring the sergeant, the Corp came over to me. "Goodbye, Pal." - "Goodbye, Corp." A long handclasp and the door closed. I was alone again.

After they had gone, I hunched down in a corner, grieving the loss of the only friend I had troubled to make since my capture, waiting for a file of guards to take me to some form of punishment. Nothing happened. At noon the door opened and the sentry left me a mess tin containing a little boiled veg.

At dusk Cohen again appeared, this time alone. "Fall in for roll-call," he ordered. "Every man gets three days' rations. The whole camp moves out in the morning." He bustled off leaving the door open. My sentry had disappeared, and I wandered out among the rest of the prisoners answering their enquiries as briefly as possible. I wasn't in the mood to be entertaining.

Yet I was uneasy and very unhappy. I found a mattress and a vacant place but having no blanket or great coat could not sleep for the cold and wandered about all night, prowling up and down like a caged wolf, trying to still my restlessness and to keep warm. Long afterwards I learned that the Corp died of pneumonia on the train.

Towards dawn I resolved to have another try for freedom. According to Cohen the whole camp was moving out. My idea was simply to hide in the prison and let the present inhabitants and their keepers go off and leave me. I would lie hidden all day and under cover of darkness have no trouble in scaling the unguarded wire.

This plan obviated the risk of a bullet, as a guard would be unlikely to fire on a prisoner who was found hiding inside the prison. There would be a row, of course. I might get roughed about a bit and some disciplinary punishment. But that would be the worst I could expect.

The moon was still dark; I had three days' rations in my pocket; the front line was less than forty miles away, and I had a murderously stiff term of punishment immediately ahead. Another get-away was undoubtedly in order.

Chapter Thirteen

This scheme was the simplest, the safest and the best of all my attempts. I knew enough of the management of the camp generally to know that we would not be called to fall in until just before the time for departure. I knew, too, that on such a morning the sergeant would have the very devil of a time getting everybody lined up. Staff men, sick paraders, fellows nipping off at the last minute to retrieve some treasure left under the mattress. The NCOs gone the previous day, plus specials like myself, would all tend to throw his books out of balance. I could easily imagine if he found himself only one man short, that he would be well satisfied. If he suspected an escape he would think it had occurred during the night.

I decided on the *Kammer* or storeroom as offering the best cover. It was usually kept locked, but I figured that some one of the staff would likely have occasion to go in there for something before they all moved out.

About daybreak a couple of guards came in and started to rouse the men. "*Raus! Raus!*" they shouted, kicking at the extended rows of feet. Groans, curses and yawns told of the awakening camp. As every man had been given three days' rations, the night before, no bread was issued this morning, though "coffee" could be had at the cookhouse. So it was not long before we got the order to fall in.

While the men were slowly forming up, I hovered back and forth in front of the Kammer. Presently Cohen unlocked the door and entered. I felt a bit suspicious of the little German-speaking Jew, but stragglers like myself were momentarily growing fewer, and it was a case of now or never. Striding boldly to the open door I walked in to meet Cohen just emerging.

"Here, where are you going?" he asked, attempting to bar my way.

"Get out of here and keep your mouth shut," I snapped tensely.

"Well, but what is the idea? What do you want in here?" he insisted.

"If you must know, I'm going to hide in here till the rest of you have gone. And now get out and leave the door unlocked." He went then, a thin little smile hovering around his mouth.

As the door closed, I glanced quickly about the room. It was lighted only by one small window high up on the side that over-looked Roll-call Alley. Opposite the window lay a good-sized heap of tattered coats and uniforms. Right under the window lay a smaller pile. I decided on the latter, as it lay in the darkest corner of the place.

Burrowing in by the wall I soon succeeded in covering myself, leaving a small passage between the heap and the wall for breathing purposes. Then I lay still. Outside I could hear Cohen and the German sergeant numbering off the parade. Presently some one came in, strolled around the Kammer and went out again. Soon after that I heard the men move off, and the camp grew silent. As the hours crept silently by, my anxieties abated, and I gradually felt more secure.

About ten o'clock I heard faint sounds in other parts of the camp. They grew more distinct, and presently someone entered my retreat. He paused inside the door, evidently looking the place over, then strolled right to my pile under the window. I was lying on my side with my face to the wall. He kicked at a garment or two, then picked up a coat, part of which covered the side of my face which lay uppermost. I lay as still as a partridge on her nest as I felt my cover moved. He did not lift the coat right off - just the side that was part of the cover over my head. He held the piece in his hand for a long moment, either looking at the material in his hand or at the fragment of white face that lay so still down by the wall. Presently he dropped the coat and walked out closing the door behind him.

My heart which had been bumping my tonsils was just settling back into place, when I heard visitors again approaching. Flinging open the door they strode in and grabbing an armful of coats, uncovered me. I stirred, yawned, stretched and scrambled up to meet a storm of excited *Deutsch* from three Germans who stood over me. Things looked black for a moment.

One had a bayonet which he half drew from the scabbard. Another swung back a heavy stick, but a mild, fatherly old chap came in just in time to grab his arm. While the storm raged, I tried to point out that I must have carelessly over-slept. But if I looked as scared as I felt, the bluff must have been a total wash-out.

The dangerous moment of discovery and capture having passed, the Germans soon cooled off and seemed quite proud of their cleverness in catching me. They then took me to the guard-house down by the main entrance where they were billeted. It appeared these three old Landstrunners had been left behind to look after the few supplies and materials left by the main camp.

They treated me well after their initial spleen had exhausted itself. One of them took me back to the cookhouse where, with a tin and a spoon I was set to filling myself on the boiled veg left over in the big caldron from the last mid-day meal. When I had eaten all I could tuck in and stagger back to the guard-house, the other two were in the midst of preparations for their own mid-day meal. The wire edge of my appetite having been somewhat dulled, my canny captors later showed no lack of hospitality in offering me a share of their own good and ample rations.

They kept me with them for nearly a week during which time I grew to be almost one of the family. I learned a lot of German. They never wearied of getting me to talk of overseas. These three musketeers with myself as a reluctant D'Artagnan had a very pleasant time while guarding the late prison camp. We played cards - a four-handed game something like pedro - we talked, we read, we ate from the stores they were supposed to be guarding and we slept.

They fixed me up very well with a first-rate bed and mattress and plenty of blankets in a room all to myself down in the basement. One day I found an old set of men's underwear which I washed and used as pyjamas at night. I even got some hot water in a tin and had a sponge bath down there.

They often went on foraging expeditions up into the village and around the countryside. When on trips of this sort they usually took me along on the principle, I suppose, that I could be looked after as well that way as any other. One day I found an English *Primer of Logic* in an old billet. From then on, when other entertainments palled, I delved into the mysteries of syllogisms and propositions which if they were not thrilling were at least engrossing.

The order came to clear the whole district. Trains were not to be had, nor motor vehicles. The people had no horses, cows or even dogs. The amount each person could take with him was limited to his own personal strength.

It is hard for Westeners to understand the bitter tragedy of an evacuation of that sort. To us it is our heritage that we pull stakes and move on after we have been in one place a few years or a generation or so. To European peasant standards, any people of less than twenty years' standing in a community are foreigners and outsiders. Certainly anyone who changes his place of residence every five or ten years is considered a fly-by-night and anything but a respectable citizen.

I once knew a girl in an estaminet near Bruay who was nineteen years old, and she solemnly assured me she had never visited the nearest village less than two miles away. Her name was Leonie and she had the bluest of blue eyes and the softest and waviest of dark hair. Her voice was strangely deep and husky. Oh, well... .

But as I was saying, everybody had to get out, and for those civilians it was a real event. Births, marriages and deaths were commonly to be expected of life, but to leave their homes containing their furniture, their best clothes, the vegetables they had stored for the winter, their well-worn hoes and tools, the treasured nicknacks on the chiffonier - *ah, non, ce n'est pas possible!*

But a squad of Germans came round to every house. "*Raus! Raus,*" they shouted and made sure that every person was in the street. By noon of the last day every soul had to be out of that area, and the clearing-out squad was kept busy.

My Landstrunners had made arrangements to have their chattels transported to Boussu, a town about fifteen miles east by a working camp of Russian prisoners who were also moving out, lock, stock and barrel. All the impedimenta of the Russian camp was loaded upon two huge French farm wagons - and such wagons! We never see their like back home. Wheels five feet high; hubs as big as a small man's body; tires six inches wide and an inch thick; weight, around a ton and a half; not a small nail in the whole edifice; built before the Revolution; still sound and good for another century or two of use.

171

The Russians were moving back into Germany taking the two wagons with their piled-up loads along. And by that I do not mean they were driving horses which would take the loads to Germany. Ten men to a side on two ropes tied to the end of the short stub tongue furnished the motive power.

"*Raus, Rusky, raus*," shouted the German sergeant in charge. "*Raus, raus!*" in exactly the same tone that I would use to my team back on the farm. There were not enough Russians to spell one another off, and their escort allowed them five minutes rest every hour.

My guard followed along behind as did also the Russian sergeant. I soon picked up with the latter - he could speak quite a bit of French and asked me how it came I was the only Britisher left in the Fresnes camp.

I told him I had tried to get away and asked him if he had ever done the same. In most emphatic terms he assured me he never had and moreover never intended to. It was all right for me to pull off tricks of that sort but a very different matter for the Russians. In addition to the usual punishment of short rations, pack drill and solitary confinement, they would be severely flogged, and anyone who repeatedly gave trouble would be flogged and run to death!

Poor Ruskies. As soon as the Armistice of November 11th was signed, the German soldiery, including the guards of all prison camps simply dropped their rifles and went home. British, Serbian, Italian, French, Romanian and Russian prisoners immediately, with the instinct of homing pigeons, also started for home. Of all these the Russians had the longest journey and the hardest possible conditions to overcome.

Shortly after we left Fresnes, the sky clouded over, and it began to rain, continuing so more or less steadily all day. As far as we could see through the grey drizzle the narrow road ahead was dotted with little groups of "evacuees." In spite of the heavy loads

172

and the bad roads the Russians made good time and as they were overtaken, the civilians were compelled to make way by stepping off into the mud by the roadside.

I will never forget the sights and sounds I heard that day. Nothing I had previously experienced touched me as did the sight of those people we passed. Chiefly women and children - the able-bodied men had long since been sent off to work in the mines. Only the feeble and sick and old were left of the men.

One sick woman was being carried in a great wheelbarrow by two girls, each girl lifting an arm. The empty barrow alone would have made a heavy load for them over that road.

Pitiful figures humped beneath their bundles. Wavering old couples holding one another to the road as long as they could, then sinking to the soggy ditchside when they were too exhausted to go farther.

"*Raus, raus!*" shouted the Germans, urging them on. Water dripped from the over-hanging branches of the roadside poplars. Beads of moisture hung from every dead weed and grass blade. Children cried steadily with the cold and the wet.

A woman pushed a perambulator with her few possessions, with one hand, and carried a child of four or five on her other arm.

"*Raus, raus!*"

I took the child from her while the Russian sergeant pushed the tiny conveyance. We could only help her for a few hundred yards as the woman was too exhausted to keep up. While she struggled along beside us she told me she and the child had left Fresnes the previous day but they had made only about three miles. They had slept all night in a deserted barn . . . No, they had no blankets. They were too heavy and she had thrown them away . . . They had been told to go to Brussels . . . No, she knew no one at Brussels nor anywhere along the way. Neither did she know what she would do when she got there . . . Yes, she had some money, forty-eight francs.

Suddenly, "Pardon messieurs, you go too fast for me. You must leave us." As we left her standing there in the mud beside the road with all she had left in the world, she voiced the utter grief and misery of all her kind. *"Malheur, M'sieur, malheur!"*

While waiting for our connection on the square at Mons I did very well. A number of people came up and gave me bread which I stored away for the lean days ahead. Others gave me tobacco and cigars. The latter I shared diplomatically with my three musketeers in return for which they looked intently in the opposite direction if someone approached who looked promising but timid. One woman, a refugee, gave me a large piece of salt horse. A little of this went a long way, but after a couple of days my commissariat department was disinclined to be critical, and I was very glad of it despite the fact that Dobbin must have done a mighty lot of hard work in his time to have grown so tough.

Between Mons and Soignies a lady and her daughter across the aisle of the train spoke to me. It appeared they also came from Fresnes. They lived in the Chateau Blanc which overlooked the village. Like most of the French they feared and hated the Germans intensely, but we soon worked out a system of communication which provided me with some valuable information.

As dusk fell we arrived at Soignies, and the Corporal enquired his way to the camp which was located in what had been the centre of the town's chief industry - a huge glove factory. As we approached it we met no less a personage than my dear old friend Hindenburg the camp Kommandant. When I recognized his great fat jowls and murderous expression I groaned to think of what we were about to receive; oh Lord, he wouldn't leave more of me than a smear of strawberry jam on the footpath.

The corporal saluted and reported. "Also this prisoner whom we found hiding in the Kammer after the Kommando had vacated."

At this Hindenburg spun round to inspect the insect before squashing him. Peering down into my face and recognizing me he simply exploded. *"Gott in Himmell!"* he began, but choked there. Words seemed to fail him. He opened his mouth to begin again. No go. And then - he laughed!

He laughed and laughed. Mighty guffaws that echoed up and down the empty street. Finally, giving his thumb a double jerk over his shoulder in the direction he had just come from he at once pointed the way, dismissed us and relieved my mind of a very heavy load. "Weird fish!" I thought to myself, heaving a heartfelt sigh of relief.

Inside the gate I was turned loose among the other prisoners and I bedded down for the night in a dark corner behind a steam boiler. The boiler, of course, was cold, and so was I, but there was no way of helping it.

The next morning the camp buzzed with excitement. Rumour had it that negotiations for an armistice were afoot. True or not, the story had one good effect as far as my own case was concerned. I was not called to answer for my sins, and by the time the armistice rumour had definitely proven to be a fizzle, the Kommando was moved to Germany.

Living conditions in the glove factory were the worst I had ever experienced. Less than half of us had mattresses. Only a few had a blanket or overcoat and no one had both. Water was strictly limited. Once a day a water cart came into the camp and each man could get a small tinful - if he had a tin, and until the cart was empty. If he was too far down the line to click, it was just too bad until next day. One could frequently beg a drink from someone more fortunate, but he was certainly out of luck so far as getting enough water for a wash.

Practically all of us were suffering from hunger and dysentery and there were no lavatories or latrines. In our part of the prison there were no proper rooms or sections for sleeping. One curled himself

175

up wherever he could find a fairly clean unoccupied spot. Day and night were hideous with the groans and stench from tortured bodies.

Perhaps our condition can be, to some extent, imagined. I find it difficult at this time to lash my mind into a reconstruction of the unspeakable sights and impressions carved into my soul during the five horrible days we passed in the glove factory. For food I got along a good deal better than most. George, the corporal, often smuggled me a little stew from his own mess. I still had a few marks left over and once or twice was able to buy a mess tin of potatoes or a piece of cheese from a German through the wire. Fires were forbidden, but to boil a piece of salt horse and two or three spuds without showing either light or smoke, was easy for an old front line hand. For fuel I used grease and oil scraped from the bearings of the machinery. An old piece of burlap cut into short lengths made a wick for my tiny cooker.

The guards at this camp seemed particularly regimental and strictly forebade civilians giving us food while outside the prison gates. Consequently when men were wanted for fatigue our motto was; "*Nix arbeit!*" (No work).

One trip outside convinced me that as a method of replenishing the larder fatigue parties from this camp were out. From then on I was a wily bird and adopted the popular slogan to such good effect that never again while with the Germans was I caught for a fatigue party.

The civilians at this town were very generous. For food they sent in two American Relief biscuits per man nearly every day. The owner of the glove factory presented each man a new suit of flannel underwear for winter use, and very grateful we were to get it. The fact that many of the poor beggars were so hungry that they traded their garments to the Germans for bread did not in the least detract from the munificent gift.

I found a number of old sacks and these I tied together at the edges, to make a serviceable blanket. I left my den behind the boiler room no oftener than was necessary and when I did so I carried with me whatever food that would be worth stealing. One fellow sold or traded a gold ring for a loaf of bread but had it stolen from under his head the same night,

The peace rumours flourished for a time and then as usual died out. One day the order came for about seven hundred of us to be moved to Lemberg on the other side of Germany. This movement order gave me, as the French say, "furiously to think." We were probably destined as reinforcements to a working camp labouring in the coal or salt mines. To get away from a camp of that sort would likely be a good deal harder than anything I had yet encountered. Moreover, I reflected ruefully, the other side of Germany was a mighty long hike.

Even if the war did end during the winter, that did not necessarily mean we would be immediately repatriated, as witness the case of the Russkies. The idea of being forced to work as a sort of slave in a coal or salt mine for a year or so after peace was signed certainly did not appeal to me.

There was no time for a well-laid plan for getting away from the lager itself, and, as the entire Kommando was not moving out all at once, a repeat of my last scheme would not work. As far as I could see I was booked for a long ride to Lemberg unless I could get away from the train.

The French and British, when transporting gunfodder from one part of the line to another, use box cars as a rule. These box cars along with such information as to tare weight, gross load and so on, bear also the legend - 40 *Hommes*   8 *Chevaux*.

The Germans with their well-known efficiency, improved on the Allies' method by loading 60 *hommes* into a 40 *hommes* car. They did it by providing planks fastened in cross-wise of the car for seats. Other planks were secured as rests for our backs. Instead of being spread out all over the floor, we sat up like little men in Sunday-school, six in a row, ten rows to a car and a space in the centre between the doors for three guards.

Ah-ha, thought we, this is a bit of all right, what? Good old Germany! Nice comfy planks to sit on with backs 'an all! A cute little hole at each end of the car for ventilation and the Jerries in the middle to see we don't catch cold from having the door open.

If that ride had lasted no longer than half an hour or so, our gratitude to our captors for their consideration of our comfort would have been quite touching. After that time, however, we grew increasingly aware of the deplorable lack of upholstery on those seats and our own bony points of contact. Yet in spite of all our wriggles and groans, the first twenty hours were not so bad.

We had been given three days' rations before leaving Soignies, so we did not lack for food the first day. The next morning fully half of our number had eaten their entire food supply and started to hang around the ventilation holes and beg from every passer-by whenever the train stopped.

Before night most of the carload were standing around the hole continuously for fear of losing their places. As soon as the train commenced to slow down all hands would fight and mill for the coveted position by the square of daylight like a large herd of pigs around a very small trough.

All day long the whines and snarls and struggles went on, dying down only when it grew so late that there was no further chance of any good-natured civilian passing by.

No arrangements had been made to keep us supplied with water but the weather being cool we did not suffer greatly on this account during the first day or two. From then on, the agony of thirst was added to our other miseries. On rare occasions a mess tin of water was passed to us through the holes by a civilian. One of the guards, after we had been without water for thirty-six hours, took three or four

178

mess-tins and filled them for us at a nearby tap. On the way back to the car he was stopped by a military policeman who demanded to know by whose authority the guard had taken the water. Of course no authority was invoked, whereupon the M.P. with the officious brainlessness of his breed, insisted on the water being emptied on the ground.

The train stopped frequently, and at night we would be side-tracked and left until morning. Our guards kept the door open as much as they reasonably could for sanitary purposes but during a long run, conditions in the car got pretty bad - our health being what it was.

I felt sorry for the two Germans. They did their best for us. They were almost as much prisoners as we were, and I hesitated quite a while before I finally decided to break away from them. I sincerely hoped they would not get into serious trouble when they reported their carload one man short.

Estimating as well as I could the number of hours we had been actually travelling and the average rate of speed we made, I figured after we had been on the train three days that we must be getting pretty close to the German frontier. I remembered, too, that a long tongue of Holland runs down between Germany and Belgium to a point close to the main railroads crossing the frontier.

Late that afternoon we passed through a large town. While the train stopped I had tried to find out the name of it from a civilian who was giving the fellows at the window a bit of bread. The row going on was so great that I was not sure what he said, though it sounded like Liege.

In any case I was certain of one thing - I had been on that train long enough! Even if I were recaptured within half an hour I would be no worse off unless they tied me behind and made me run the rest of the way. My experience had been that a privately conducted tour was much to be preferred to one with the common herd.

Shortly after we left the town we were side-tracked in a hilly, wooded part of the country just as it began to get dark. The snarling and quarrelling continued unceasingly, each having appreciation only for his own misery.

The stench and filth were overpowering. My skin crawled with lice which had come to me from overstocked sections adjoining. My food was about done, the only thing left being a half pound or so of salt Dobbin. I had whittled away at this from time to time during the day and though I was frantically thirsty, I did not suffer greatly from hunger.

The thought of what that mob would be like after they had travelled for another week through Germany where they could not get hand-outs from the population was not pleasant to contemplate.

As it grew darker I bequeathed my remaining horse meat and the overcoat old George had yanked from my face to the rather decent kid who sat next to me. I told him I had had enough of it.

When it was quite dark and the men prepared to make themselves as comfortable as possible for the night, I leaned over and whispered to my companion: "Come to the door with me and stand close. If I suddenly disappear don't gawp around but come back quietly and say nothing."

"I think I understand," he answered.

We scrambled over to the entrance and as my good luck would have it, the guard who had been outside with one or two men re-entered the car with them. When we signified that we wanted to get down he nodded his permission and stood in the doorway, doubtless thinking he could watch us as well from there.

As he stood to one side for us a dozen questions leaped to my mind. Did he have a shell in the barrel? Was his safety catch off? Was he quick-witted? Good on sharpshooting? How far could I run straight ahead before starting to dodge . . . ? As my feet hit the ground it flashed through my mind that I could eliminate a lot of hazard by simply dodging under the train.

180

Chapter Fourteen

Without an instant's hesitation I whirled and ducked beneath the car leaving my seat mate standing there. As I emerged on the other side, no shout warned me that my disappearance had been noticed. I judged I was safe for the moment, as men were coming and going in ones and twos all the time.

Hugging the shelter of the train, I stole along in the direction of the engine until I heard steps scuffling the cinders ahead of me. I crawled beneath and lay there flat on my back, expecting every instant the engine would start up and scrape me along with it. The man passed on, and I lost no time in crawling out again and crossing several sets of tracks to where another row of cars stood.

I felt properly away now and the next thing was to put as many miles between that prison train and me as fast as I could.

The siding I was on seemed to be surrounded by water which made it bad for a start, as all bridges on a road like this would certainly be guarded. As I stood in the shadow of the string of cars debating the matter with myself, another train from the west steamed into the yard and slowed down as it passed through. It appeared to be a passenger train laden with troops, the cars being all of the long Pullman type seen only on the crack runs in Europe. All the carriages were lighted but one, and as it glided by me, I saw my chance to get out of the yards unchallenged. Suddenly dashing forward I leaped and grasped the hand-rail at the rear of the car. But as I swung myself aboard there appeared at the open window in the door the head of a German officer.

For a second I hesitated whether or not to throw myself backward, then, as he did not seem wildly excited over his discovery, I assumed he had not recognized me as a Britisher. However, I had no intention of sticking around there under his nose and hand over hand I climbed around the end of the coach, past the buffers and on to the next coach. As I again appeared the German watched me silently.

By this time we were out of the yards and the train clipped along at a good rate. After passing through a tunnel where I was nearly smothered by smoke I noticed the German had gone from the window. Probably he had only gone in out of the smoke but I was not taking any chances and when next the train slowed down a little on the curve overlooking a high embankment, I jumped.

Over and over I rolled to the bottom; nettles, brambles and rocks all leaving their mark on my hide. I sat for a minute to unscramble my addled senses. Then, taking my direction from the moon which was high and full, I struck out in a northerly direction.

Oh, but it was good to get out of that stinking snarling, hell on wheels and to be free once more! At the first ditch of water I lay and drank my fill, then washed my filthy hands and face. For a little I lay stretched out on the moist, sweet-smelling earth watching the stars swinging high overhead. I drank in great lungfuls of the pure, clean night air, deeply luxuriating in the beauty of the evening.

Past experiences had taught me that the civilian population could be absolutely relied upon to lend all possible aid to an escaping prisoner. With this fact in mind I resolved to make enquiries as to my exact whereabouts at once and on gaining what appeared to be a well-travelled road I lay down in the shelter of a hedge to await someone who could give me the information.

After a little, a young couple came strolling along and being reassured by the white collar the man was wearing that he was a civilian, I stepped forward and asked them how far it was to the Holland frontier. They replied it was eighteen kilometres - about ten miles - straight north.

I thanked them and was turning away, when they asked me if I were British. My reply put them in a great furore of excitement. It appeared that particular area was one huge German camp, and they promptly hurried me into a house a few yards down the road where no Germans were billeted.

Here, behind carefully shielded windows, together with the bachelor occupant of the house, we went into session to debate the next step. But first my host brought out some bread and meat which was very acceptable.

They were emphatic in objecting to my avowed intention of crossing the frontier. They said it was now almost an impossible feat as the Germans had a triple belt of barbed wire entanglements all along the boundary. This wire was, moreover, electrified, and guards at intervals of less than one hundred yards continually patrolled between their posts.

I pointed out that I had heard of others getting across and didn't see why I could not do the same. They agreed that many people had indeed crossed earlier in the war, but during the last year or two the Germans had put a stop to that with their electrification of the wire. They thought the safest and therefore the best thing to do was to hide somewhere until the war was over.

I laughed politely at this suggestion - it seemed so unthinkable - but they assured me that the papers were full of peace rumours again, and that possibly an armistice would be arranged within two or three weeks.

This put a different complexion on the matter. I would much rather sleep out in the woods for a while than take a chance with an electrified wire.

One of them mentioned that Soumagne, a village about half way up to Holland, was off the main route of traffic and no Germans were billeted there. Monsieur Dancel, the village baker was a good man and would help me decide what to do.

So they hunted me up a suit of civilian clothes to pull over my khaki in case I met any of the enemy, and providing me with a note to the baker, they escorted me well out of the village and on to the road where we parted company.

With no difficulty I found the village of Soumagne and though I followed right along the road I met no Germans. This fact indicated the value of the judgement of my Belgian friends.

It was about midnight when I peered up at the signboard over a shuttered shop and read thereon "*P. Dancel, Boulanger.*" No light was showing - nor anywhere in the village, so rather than disturb the good folk I found an old cart in which I curled up for the night. But it was too cold to sleep and after an hour or so I gave up the effort and walked up and down the silent lanes until morning.

As the letter I had brought was unsigned, the baker, an elderly stout man, was at first suspicious of a trap but he took me into the kitchen at the rear, and while I was eating some breakfast, brought in a lady who could speak better English than I could French. It didn't take her long to be convinced that I was a genuine specimen of an escape, and she soon reassured the baker and his family.

Their opinion about attempting to cross the frontier agreed with that of my friends in the last village. It was, they said, impossible to cross and meant almost certain death to try. They strongly urged me to stay with them in the village. Three French soldiers were also in hiding there already and as a convincing argument they brought in one of the Frenchmen to tell me his experiences.

I hated to give up my idea of going home by the most direct route; moreover I disliked accepting the charity of those good people. The stout baker finally settled my last objection by offering me a job for my board in the bake-room.

After I had been working in the bakery for a couple of weeks I was awakened one night by the roar of several heavy cars as they sped through the village. I turned over, sleepily wondering what was going on at that hour of the night.

Next morning Madame, the baker's wife, brought in the news that the Kaiser Wilhelm had abdicated and that he and his staff had passed through the village the night before on their way to Holland. I smiled politely at the story, though of course no crazy village pump rumour of that sort could get a rise out of me.

One morning M. Dancel waddled into the bake room where I was helping to get the dough into the pans, and announced that the Belgian flag was flying from the church steeple. Everyone in the house hurried to the door. Sure enough, a red, yellow and black Belgian flag! Could it be - It must be - peace! They would never dare hoist it otherwise.

All down the street the people stood at their doors and gazed on the miracle. A few walked down to the church for more information, though I was too sceptical to take the chance.

The armistice rumour persisted however, and about eleven o'clock the church bell began to toll and continued for an hour or so. When it ceased I peeped from the door again more than half expecting to see that the flag had been torn down by a squad of furious Germans. To my incredulous view, however, several more Belgian flags were in sight.

Armistice? Peace at last? Well, maybe, but I wasn't going to take any foolish chances yet. After the bread was out I donned my civvies and hit off for the next town to learn if they had heard anything about it.

In a quiet estaminet on a side street my cautious enquiries elicited the information that an armistice had actually been signed that day at eleven o'clock.

It was true! It must be true! Yet I walked back soberly enough vainly trying to realize that the war was really and truly over, and that a *feld-grau* uniform was no longer to be feared and hated.

Next day I struck across country and visited Liege. News had come through that the town had gone mad with joy. I still felt sceptical enough to hold to my disguise, though my first glimpse of the hysterically joyous city was enough to sweep away my last cautious doubts.

Crowds thronged the streets, the guests of honour being the local camp of British war-prisoners who had walked out when their guards abandoned their posts the day before. In all the restaurants and estaminets they were being wined, dined, cigared and womaned in the most regal style.

I wandered around and looked on quietly for an hour or so but being neither fish nor fowl to outward appearances, I felt somewhat out of touch, so came back to my diggings in the village and prepared for departure.

On every road and lane great numbers of Germans, in small groups of from two to a dozen men, straggled eastward, wearily dragging their possessions on machine-gun hand carts or wheelbarrows, little scraps of red cloth in their caps or pinned to their grey tunics.

Peace! Peace! Without the last lingering shadow of a doubt.

That night I uncovered my old uniform and gave it a good brush-up. Madame ironed my puttees until they looked fairly neat and tidy. I felt so enthusiastic I even gave the old brass buttons a bit of a shine. I was going home! Next morning after bidding my hospitable friends farewell, I hit out in a north-westerly direction, headed for the sea and England.

I met thousands of Germans, for the most part in

proper column of route, singing cheerfully as they swung along. Going along that morning I kicked up more disturbance than I had hitherto created in all my life before. As I approached a village some one would catch sight of my khaki in the distance. *"Les Anglais. Les Anglais!"* would be the cry and by the time I came up, everybody, his wife, his kids and his dogs were out on the street to stare at me.

If I showed the slightest inclination to stop and enquire my way, I would be swamped with offers of beer, coffee, food and lodging for a month.

The weather was glorious - what we ourselves would call Indian Summer - but even if it had poured with rain I don't think it would have made much difference to me. I WAS GOING HOME! In those four simple words lay the culmination of nearly four years of homesick longing. At last - at long last - I was going home.

I did not care a single hoot as to who had won the war - the main thing was that it was over, and that now I could go home and be rid forever of the hateful system which dictated one's every movement: the hour one went to bed - got up; which town one should visit and which was "out of bounds;" what one should write to his girl; how he must fasten his shoelaces; how he must stand, look and speak in the exalted presence of someone in a different style of uniform.

Never again would I feel the gnaw and ache of the packstraps biting into my shoulders. Never more that dread, insidious drowsiness of outraged nature, when to yield might mean death from a trench dagger or a firing squad of one's fellows. Never more to live intimately with men whose every other word was a smear of filth. Never again would I be compelled to drive my bayonet into the vitals of a man I had never before met.

The war was over! I was through. My own man at last - to live and love and work out my own destiny in the manner that I thought best. The war was finished, and I was going home.

That afternoon I passed a column of infantry that

lay resting beside the road. They stared curiously, and the usual good-humoured barrage of wisecracks in German, English and soldier-French was aimed at me. At the end of the column a little knot of officers stood talking. They fell silent as I drew near and eyed me with a careless interest. The face of one seemed oddly familiar, and as I tried to place him in my memory I saw him nod in my direction and make some remarks to the others of which the only word I caught was "Schummerly."

At the name, I stopped dead before them and looked at the speaker intently. It was Heinrich, the chap in the pyjamas, whose rest the Corp and I had disturbed twice in the same night. "Pardon me, sir," I said, saluting, "I heard you speak of Schummerly. Could you tell me where I could find him?"

They stared at me coldly for a moment, then one answered in very good English, "The Hauptmann Schummerly was killed at Mons the night before the Armistice."

"Killed? The night before the Armistice?" I echoed stupidly.

He nodded and went on, "He was trying to find out if your men intended to take the town before the Armistice was signed next day. Our men were exhausted, and we wanted to avoid further slaughter .

"Near a small bridge the Hauptmann suddenly encountered one of your men. He flashed his light upon him and fired first. The sentry dropped and more of your men ran up and surrounded Schummerly, firing as they came. They kept shooting into his body after he was dead. The corporal who followed him and saw the occurrence, said they were men from your country."

While I stared at him, dumb, a whistle blew. The men scrambled wearily to their feet, formed up and resumed their march. By the dusty roadside I stood and watched them disappear, the tiny red symbols of the revolution bobbing about crazily from their slung rifles. Soon, I turned and plodded on.

188

Chapter Fifteen

About noon of the following day I came into the ancient walled town of Tongres. While I was enquiring my way, a well dressed youth of sixteen and his English speaking sister, a golden haired little beauty of eighteen, invited me to their home for dinner. They took me to a huge mansion on the main boulevard. Over the dinner table the entire family united in their efforts to persuade me to stay and await the arrival of the troops. Their argument was that by remaining as their guest until the trains were again in operation, I would get to England just as soon and save myself a long walk. Two or three smiles from Louise, the girl who spoke English, in support of this view completely upset my previous intentions. The end of the matter being that I stayed.

They treated me royally. My bedroom was a symphonic dream in white and blue and gold; lace-hung bed curtains, full length mirrors, French windows opening upon a roof garden.

Many an hour in company with Louise or Emile, the boy, I sat in the window seat of the Petit Salon watching the seemingly endless files of field-grey as they swung singing past to the eastward. But gradually the numbers thinned, then ceased entirely. The Town Kommandant and his staff moved out, and the long, white road was empty.

As soon as the last vestiges of military authority had vanished, the townsfolk tore down the many sign-boards and notices in German - hated symbols of a hated rule - and held a joyous bonfire with them on the public square. People who had been friendly with the invaders, especially women, were hunted down like rats and their hair cropped short to their heads. They were then banished from the city and their homes looted.

* * *

A few days later the Belgian troops arrived. First came a solitary cavalryman - a lancer - clip-clopping proudly down the centre of the street. The news flashed through the town, and the crowd of excited citizens, wild with joy, that immediately gathered almost mobbed the fellow. As his horse gently forced its way along, many women crowded forward to kiss his dusty stirrup or coat.

At the Mairie he delivered word that on the following day at twelve sharp the division that had gone to the war from this area would arrive home. This, I thought, was a very generous concession to sentiment on the part of the military authorities.

And then such a bustling hither and yon! Such a search for Belgian and Allied flags so long hidden from view. In a neighbouring field the town band began to practice the long forbidden *"streng verboten"* Belgian national anthem and the *Marseillaise*.

A messenger was sent to meet the advancing troops carrying an invitation to two generals to dine "en famille" with my hosts. The huge brass and crystal chandelier from its secret hiding place under the stairs was carefully exhumed and re-hung in its proper place in the Grande Salon. From the garden heavy sacks of brass and copper door knobs, window and dresser handles were unearthed, polished and screwed back into their original places.

Next morning shortly after eleven every person in the town assembled around the cobble stoned square in the shadow of the old, old cathedral.

It was not a happy crowd that collected there. Most were too apprehensive for joy as yet. Even for those who had no close or personal interest in the returning unit, feeling was much too intense for joy. The home-coming of the troops signified in such a tangible manner the definite end of the long iron-handed oppression which had ruled them.

But now the field-grey hordes had gone. Peace had come at last and in her wake the little army of loved ones, long banished. Four weary years of heartsick longing; four years of aching anxiety; four years of slavery; four years of mud and blood and death. But the end was at hand. Hopes would soon be realized or forever shattered.

At last they appeared! Headed by the town band - they might have been playing the *Marseillaise,* but no one could hear the music for the cheers. Pelted with a storm of flowers, about twenty-five horsemen formed up around the square coming to a halt facing the centre.

Then came the infantry, numbering perhaps two hundred. The flowers and the cheers! With shrieks of joy some woman by the roadside would recognize her own particular soldier and rush forward to get a preliminary hug and kiss. Inside the hollow square made by the cavalry the infantry formed up in columns of platoons.

But where are the rest? An entire division went away! Where are the others? I could hear the queries growing momentarily more anxious and grief-laden. I could see the dread question asked in many an eager watching eye that scanned the now empty avenue.

For those who failed to find the one they sought, there was still the hope that he might have been wounded and was in hospital. As a result, when the men were paraded to their headquarters and dismissed, the sudden rush of women nearly swept them from their feet.

Where was Georges? In hospital with a bullet through his knee.

Jacques and Henri? Blown to pieces by the same shell.

Gaston? In hospital. Wounded? How badly? Shell-shocked and insane.

Alphonse? Blinded at the Marne.

Then from the men: What of Celeste? Why is she not here to greet me? Is she ill? Died of grippe last month.

What of Finette and Lucie? Banished, their hair cut.

Malheur! *Malheur*!

I turned away.

* * *

I found my regiment late one night in Mons. One of the few men left that I knew took me to his billet and bedded me down for the night.

Of course I had to give a brief account of my adventures. Then he in turn told me of all the doings I had missed since my capture. We talked and talked until weariness began to assert itself. Conversation flagged, and I was just on the point of dropping off to sleep when Roy said, "You remember Moose Mooreton whose brother was killed at Sanctuary Wood in '16?"

I roused slightly. "Sure, how's ol' Moose gettin' on?"

"Moose had the rottenest luck. He was killed right here at Mons the night before the Armistice."

"Killed at Mons the night before the Armistice?" I echoed, a ghostly feeling that I had said that before somewhere flashing through my mind.

"Yeah, you remember he was wounded at Regina Trench in '16. Well, he got back just in time to catch all the dirt during the past couple of months. We

192

were rushing Fritz as hard as we could for days and we got to the outskirts of this town the night of November 10th. Moose was on picket duty out in front when a German officer suddenly flashed a light on him and shot him dead.

I heaved to a sitting posture, the blanket falling from my shoulders. Although I knew the rest of the story I could not forbear asking, "And the German officer, did he - get away?"

"Ho-ho, I should say not," scoffed Roy, the theological student. "The rest of Moose's party ran up and sure made a thorough job of killing that Boche. They kept on shooting until after he had stopped wiggling."

I sat there staring into the darkness for a long moment.

* * *

Spring had come again, and the new wheat was green when I arrived home. Mother and Dad and the whole neighbourhood were there at the station to greet me. Such a fuss they made. Speeches, receptions and more speeches. In Belgium and France and England and on the boat coming home and everywhere the train stopped. And even now after we were home. Speeches!

Yet it was good to be one of the heroes of the day and to learn that I'd had a part in saving civilization. Ours had not been just another war. It was definitely the last! While actually at the front I had lost sight of these high motives, being more concerned in the immediate job in hand, which usually was to keep out of sight as much as possible. However, it was all over now, and my four years of war had borne truly noble fruit - Peace!

And such a peace. Not for a year or a decade, but forever! I hoped Eddie Heath and all the other fellows whose dying heads I had pillowed on my thighs were looking down and listening. They, I knew, would be glad to hear their lives had not been thrown away needlessly. Ed Heath's widow and his two children would, I thought, be comforted to know that their sacrifice was to benefit all future humanity.

We had won the Great War! Everything would be all right now. No more tyrants. Yes, everything would be perfect.

ISBN 155212427-4

9 781552 124277